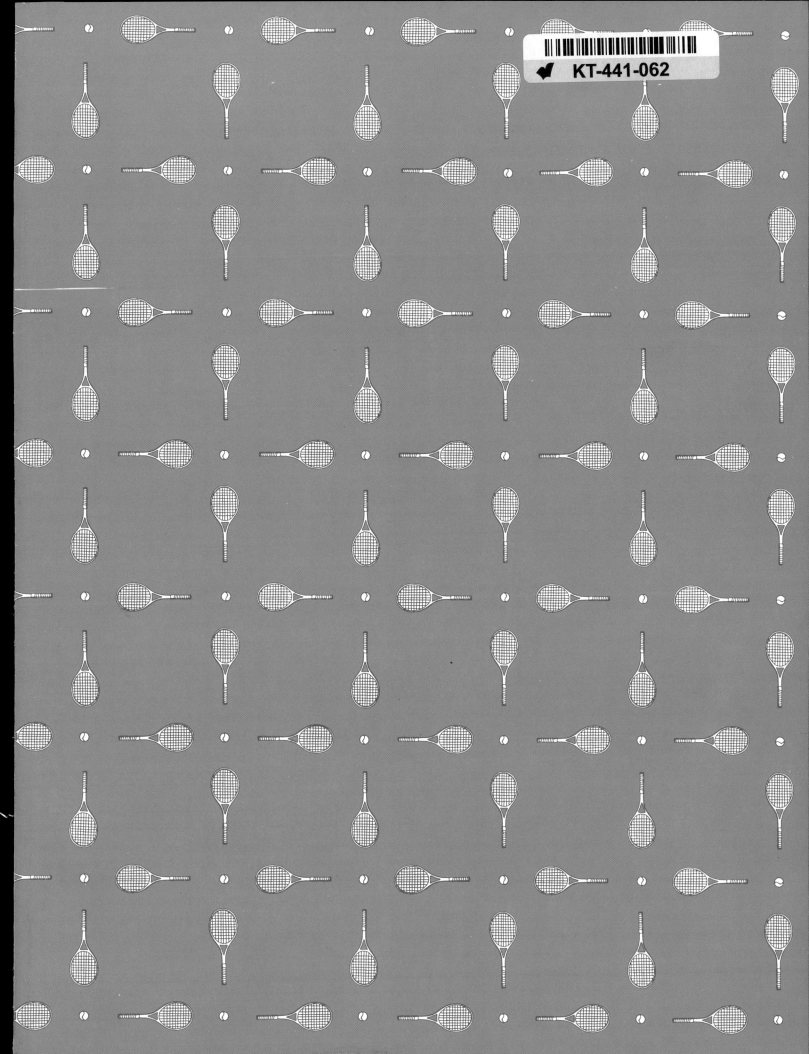

EYEWITNESS ◉ GUIDES

SPORT

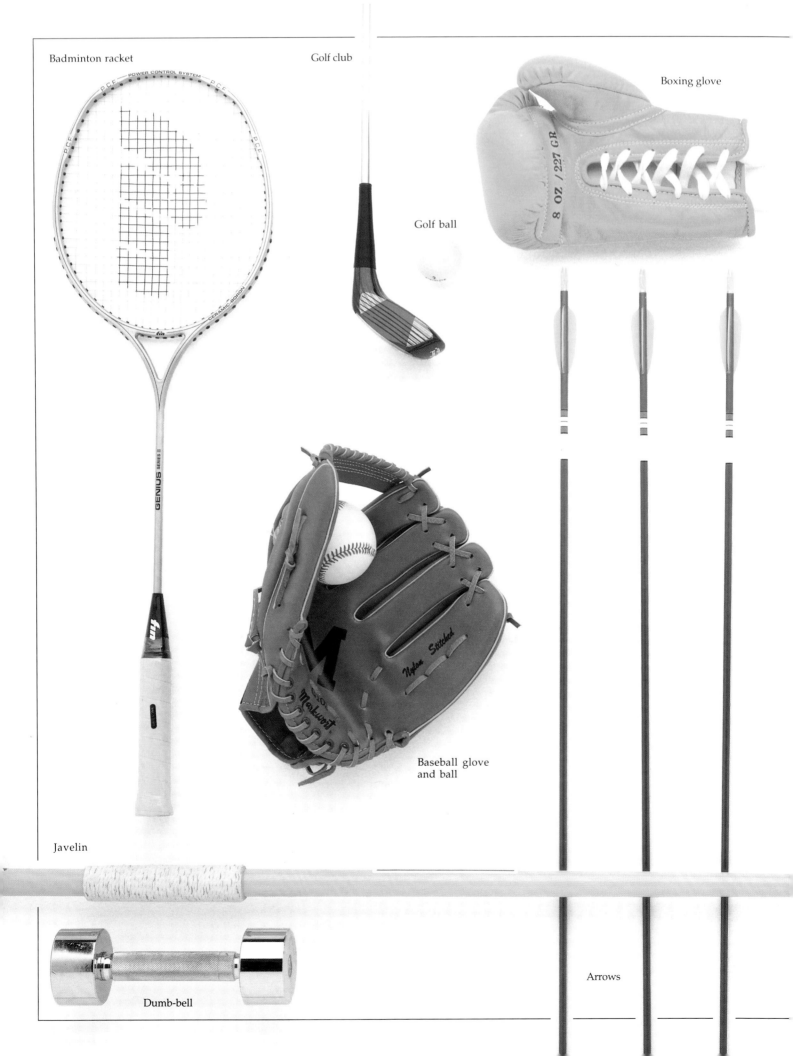

Badminton racket

Golf club

Boxing glove

Golf ball

Baseball glove
and ball

Javelin

Dumb-bell

Arrows

Starting pistol

EYEWITNESS ◉ GUIDES

SPORT

Cricket batting glove

Written by
TIM HAMMOND

American football

Rubber running-track granules

Shuttlecocks

Shot

Relay batons

Stopwatch

DORLING KINDERSLEY • LONDON

Tennis ball

Shuttlecock

Hockey stick

Referee's whistle

Project editor Tim Hammond
Art editor Mike Clowes
Managing editor Vicky Davenport
Managing art editor Jane Owen
Special photography Dave King

Conceived by Editions Gallimard
and Dorling Kindersley

First published in Great Britain in 1988
by Dorling Kindersley Limited,
9 Henrietta Street, London WC2E 8PS

Reprinted 1989, 1990, 1991

Pool balls

Dart

Golf tees

Measuring tape

British Library Cataloguing in Publication Data
Sport. - (Eyewitness).
    1. Sports
    I. Series
    796

ISBN 0-86318-317-4

Colour reproduction by Colourscan, Singapore
Typeset by Windsor Graphics, Ringwood, Hampshire
Printed in Italy by A. Mondadori Editore, Verona

Squash ball

Headband

Spiked track shoes

Contents

Soccer boot studs

Cricket ball

Soccer

SOCCER IS A TEAM SPORT in which players attempt to score goals by kicking or "heading" a ball into the opposing team's goal. Except for the goalkeeper, and when taking throw-ins, the players are not allowed to touch the ball with their hands or arms. Games in which a ball is kicked have been played around the world in various forms for centuries: soldiers in ancient China played "football" as part of their army training - using the head of an enemy warrior as the ball! In medieval England, the sport was banned by the king because men preferred it to practising their archery, and many were so badly injured in the violent matches that they were not fit to fight in the army. Soccer is one of a group of sports - including American football and rugby - that grew out of these early "games". Perhaps more than any other sport, it has always been seen as "the game of the people" and is still the most popular sport in the world, played and watched by millions.

THE FIFA WORLD CUP
The top soccer-playing nations compete for this cup every four years. The original World Cup was kept by Brazil in 1970, after they had won it three times.

Bright-coloured fabric can be seen clearly under floodlights

Linesman's flag

THE FIELD OF PLAY
The first soccer matches were played in the streets; there were no time limits - in fact, very few rules at all! Landmarks - such as the gates of the village church - were used as goals. Modern matches are contested by teams of 11 players.

Corner flag

Centre circle

Penalty area

Half-way line

Goalposts

Penalty spot

ON THE LINES
Two linesmen patrol the length of the field, assisting the referee. They use flags to signal when the ball goes out of play, or when players have broken the rules of the game.

MAN IN THE MIDDLE
The referee starts and stops play by blowing his whistle. Yellow and red cards are held up to show when a player has been cautioned or sent off.

"W-M" formation

TEAM FORMATIONS
Each team may organize its defenders, midfield, and attacking players in a different way.

"4-4-2" formation

PLAYING TIME
Two "halves" of 45 minutes each are played. The referee may add on extra time if the game has been delayed.

Red card

Referee's whistle

Yellow card

Football fashions

The modern soccer player's clothing has changed greatly from that worn by the first professionals over a hundred years ago. In 1875, players had not started wearing numbers on their shirts. The kit of each player was different from that of his teammates so that he could be identified by the colour of his cap or his stockings! Perhaps the most drastic change has been in footwear: the clumsy "armoured" boots of the last century have evolved gradually into the supple and sophisticated modern shoes that are now only a third as heavy.

1880s *above*
At this time it was normal to kick the ball with the toe, so boots were made with steel or chrome toe-caps to protect the kicker's feet. Pads were worn outside the stockings to protect shins against stray kicks!

Leather sole

1930s-1950s
Despite the baggy shorts, the player's kit was now lighter, although the boots still weighed around 500 g (1 lb) each.

More streamlined shape

Mid-20th century boots

Boots reached above the ankle

Early-20th century boots

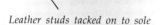

Leather studs tacked on to sole

THE GOALKEEPER
The goalkeeper is the only player allowed to handle the ball. He wears a different-coloured shirt to the other players, and many also wear gloves to help them grip the ball, and peaked caps to shade their eyes from the sun.

ARTIFICIAL GRASS
Grass pitches get very wet and boggy during the winter, so some teams play on pitches made from synthetic materials that are unaffected by the weather. However, artificial pitches are more common in American football (p. 10).

1980s *below*
Modern soccer boots weigh only about 250 g (8 oz) or less. The development of such light and supple shoes went hand-in-hand with changing playing styles; as footballers became more skilful, they needed shoes that allowed them to use their speed and ball control.

Late-20th century boots

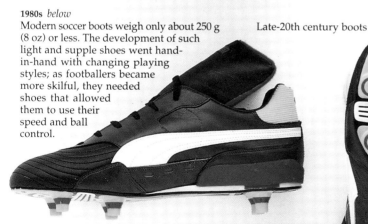

Rubber studs   *Aluminium studs*   *Nylon studs*

INTERCHANGEABLE STUDS
Studs of different materials and sizes are suitable for different pitch conditions; flat rubber studs for hard ground, aluminium for wet and slippery conditions, and nylon when the pitch is soft but firm.

"ASTRO BOOTS"
Soccer boots with interchangeable studs are unsuitable for artificial grass pitches. Instead, modified training shoes are usually worn. A pattern of tiny moulded studs or "pimples" provides the most comfortable shoe and the best grip. This shoe has 73 more "studs" than a normal soccer boot!

How soccer balls are made

Nowadays, soccer balls - as well as the balls used in some other sports - are often made from synthetic materials, moulded into the correct shape. However, the balls used by the professional teams have always been made from leather panels, stitched together around a rubber bladder, and the best balls are still made this way. Leather balls have better air resistance so they don't wobble in flight.

Untreated leather scuffed easily

Final seam had to be laced up

PRE-WAR BALL
Until the 1940s, footballs were always tan-coloured. They were not as waterproof as modern balls and so tended to become very heavy in wet conditions. The technique for stitching up the final panels of the ball was not yet invented, so these balls were always laced.

ROUGH AND TUMBLE
The early soccer matches were rowdy affairs, with teams of 100 or more charging through the streets chasing a ball made from an inflated pig's bladder.

Football in the Middle Ages

One needle is used at each end of the waxed thread

Maker's name stamped on to panels

Making a leather ball

Holes punched in panels for stitching

Edges cut to fit together perfectly

1 CUTTING THE PANELS
The leather is coated in special paint to make it waterproof, and a strong lining is stuck to the back to make the leather stiffer and stop it stretching. The firmest leather is used to make the most expensive balls; softer leather stretches more easily and is used for cheaper, practice balls. Two types of panel are cut out using special knives. There are 18 panels in this type of ball.

Threads twisted together and rubbed in wax

2 STITCHING THE PANELS TOGETHER
Now the stitcher begins to join the leather panels together, using two needles and a special waxed thread made up of five strands. The wax makes the thread waterproof and easier to use. The panels are held together in a special clamp (*see opposite*) gripped between the stitcher's knees, so he can have both hands free.

Old-fashioned ball-making tools

MINERVA SUPREME
GUARANTEED HAND SEWN
THE MINERVA® FOOTBALL CO. LTD.
ENGLAND
FIFA APPROVED

THE STITCHING HORSE
The ball-maker sits on a special bench that has a clamp that holds the leather panels tightly while he stitches them together.

These panels are for a rugby ball, which is made in a similar way to a soccer ball (p. 14)

Clamp gripped between knees

Clamp secured by adjustable metal grip

32-PANEL BALL
Balls can be made in several different ways. The main difference is in the number and shape of the panels. This ball is made with a combination of 12 five-sided and 20 six-sided panels.

Bladder valve

Bladder made from latex rubber

5-A-SIDE FOOTBALL
A ball like the one shown above is designed for indoor soccer with five or six players on each team. It is slightly smaller than a normal soccer ball, and made from soft, felt-like material that has a low bounce ideal for indoor games.

ALTERNATIVE DESIGN
The players in this 1924 match are using a ball made from just 12 panels - the fewer panels there are, the less perfectly round the ball will be.

Finished ball weighs 400-450 g (14-16 oz)

Panels sewn together with ball inside-out

The ball will be kicked and headed thousands of times throughout its life

3 FORMING THE SHAPE OF THE BALL
The seams on each set of three panels are hammered flat to make the ball as round as possible. With the ball inside-out, they are then sewn together, at right-angles to each other. The seams are hammered again to make sure the corners are smooth, and the ball is turned the right way round. The last side of the ball is partly sewn on, leaving enough room for the stitcher to push the rubber bladder into the ball. The valve of the bladder fits through a hole punched into one of the panels of the ball.

4 THE FINISHED BALL
With the ball the right way out, the stitcher begins the difficult task of sewing up the final seam. He cannot tie off the thread in a knot or it would show on the outside of the ball, so he sews it back into the ball and cuts off the ends as close as he can. The ball is given a thorough inspection to check for any faults, and is blown up with air to the correct pressure. Each ball takes about three-and-a-half hours to make.

American football

AMERICAN FOOTBALL IS an exciting sport played by two teams of 11 players, although up to 40 men can play for each team during a single match. The tactics of the game can be very complicated, but the object is simple - to score points by crossing the opponents' goal-line with the ball (a "touchdown") or by kicking the ball between their goalposts. The game is therefore based around the teams' attempts to gain ground up the field. It was first played in the American colleges in the late 19th century and is, without doubt, the team sport with the greatest amount of physical contact. The helmets and huge shoulder pads worn by the players help make this one of the most spectacular of all sports. Canadian football has slightly different rules.

Padded-up American football player in full flight

Football helmet

Face mask made from unbreakable plastic coated in rubber

SHOCK ABSORBERS *below*
Inside the helmet, cells filled with air or anti-freeze liquid help prevent injury by spreading impact evenly.

HEAD CASES
Every player must wear a proper helmet with a protective face mask. The first "helmets" were made from boiled leather, but the modern ones are tough plastic. Most players also use a gumshield to protect their teeth.

THE "GRIDIRON"
Each team has four attempts to advance 9m (10 yd) up the field - each attempt is called a "down". If they succeed, they play a further four downs, otherwise their opponents win possession of the ball. The "gridiron" pitch is marked out in yards to show how far a team has advanced.

Goal line

Hashmarks every yard

Goalpost

End zone

Numbers every 10 yards with arrows pointing to nearest goal line

Yard lines every 5 yards

MODERN WARRIORS
"Warpaint" was first worn by the Washington Redskins team. The players found that painting their cheeks in this way helped prevent glare from the sun. Other teams copied and face-paint is now a common sight.

NFL HELMETS
The names of the 28 teams in the National Football League (NFL) are made up of their city name and a nick-name. The helmets worn by the teams often bear a logo relating to their nicknames.

...AND THE ORIGINAL
The names of many football teams reflect the aggress-ive nature of the sport. Each game is like a battle, with teams advancing and retreating.

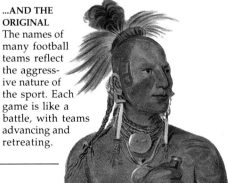

Cincinnati Bengals

Los Angeles Rams

Philadelphia Eagles

New York Jets

San Diego Chargers

Buffalo Bills

Seattle Seahawks

New York Giants

Shoulder pads

BROAD SHOULDERS
Shoulder and chest pads can weigh up to 2.5 kg (5.5 lb), depending on the position of the player.

Upper arm pads can be attached to shoulder pads

TACKLE-DUMMY
Players build strength and practice their blocking technique on this special piece of equipment.

ARM PADS
The amount of padding worn by each player depends on how fast and agile he must be to do his particular job.

Fingerless gloves give protection and freedom of movement

FOOTBALL SHIRTS
Some players wear tight-fitting shirts that are difficult for opponents to grab. Others wear shirts made of flimsy fabric that simply tears away if pulled. The numbers on the front must be at least 20 cm (8 in) high, and those on the back at least 25 cm (10 in).

Elbow pads

WHAT NUMBER?
Each team is made up of three separate groups of eleven players: the "offence", "defence", and "special" teams. Number 34 would be worn by a member of the offence.

GLOVES
Some players wear gloves, to protect their hands and help them grip the ball; others use adhesive tape.

The need for padding

Early forms of American football were very dangerous - in 1905, for example, 18 college footballers were killed and over 150 badly injured. This led to changes in the rules about protective clothing, to help make the sport safer. Many footballers use adhesive tape as a form of protection - some professional teams can use over 300 miles of tape in a season!

RIB PADS *left*
Apart from their helmets and bulky shoulder pads, players wear padding to prevent injuries to the lower parts of their body. The rib pads are like a corset with a hard plastic shell; they tie on to the shoulder pads and lace up at the front.

Straps tie on to shoulder pads

HIP AND GROIN PADS *below*
The protection for the pelvic area is made up of three separate pads - one for each hip and one for the groin. These are held together by straps that are threaded through each pad and done up at the back.

Rigid plastic covering

Foam-sponge filling

Thigh pads

Leg pads slipped under tight-fitting breeches

BREECHES *above*
The padding for the hips and legs is worn underneath close-fitting knee-length breeches which lace up at the front.

Knee pads

THE BALL

An American football is oval in shape, with pointed - rather than rounded - ends that make it easier to throw one-handed. It is made from a rubber bladder, inflated with air and covered in "pebble-grained" leather. In professional football, the home team has to provide 24 footballs for each match.

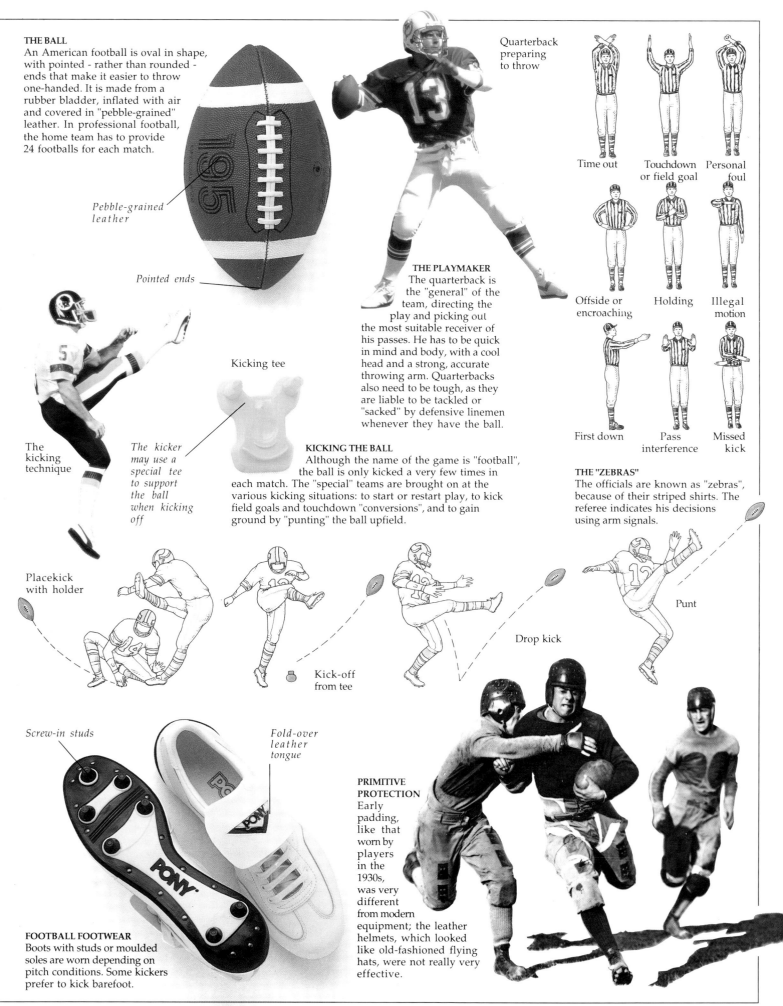

Pebble-grained leather

Pointed ends

Kicking tee

Quarterback preparing to throw

Time out

Touchdown or field goal

Personal foul

Offside or encroaching

Holding

Illegal motion

First down

Pass interference

Missed kick

The kicking technique

The kicker may use a special tee to support the ball when kicking off

THE PLAYMAKER

The quarterback is the "general" of the team, directing the play and picking out the most suitable receiver of his passes. He has to be quick in mind and body, with a cool head and a strong, accurate throwing arm. Quarterbacks also need to be tough, as they are liable to be tackled or "sacked" by defensive linemen whenever they have the ball.

KICKING THE BALL

Although the name of the game is "football", the ball is only kicked a very few times in each match. The "special" teams are brought on at the various kicking situations: to start or restart play, to kick field goals and touchdown "conversions", and to gain ground by "punting" the ball upfield.

THE "ZEBRAS"

The officials are known as "zebras", because of their striped shirts. The referee indicates his decisions using arm signals.

Placekick with holder

Kick-off from tee

Drop kick

Punt

Screw-in studs

Fold-over leather tongue

FOOTBALL FOOTWEAR

Boots with studs or moulded soles are worn depending on pitch conditions. Some kickers prefer to kick barefoot.

PRIMITIVE PROTECTION

Early padding, like that worn by players in the 1930s, was very different from modern equipment; the leather helmets, which looked like old-fashioned flying hats, were not really very effective.

Rugby

Scoring a try

RUGBY IS A SPORT in which players are allowed to carry, kick and throw the ball, although they may only throw it backwards. Points are scored by touching the ball down over the opponents' goal-line (a "try") or by kicking it over the crossbar and between the goalposts. The sport gets its name from Rugby school in England where it was first played in 1823. The "inventor" of the sport was William Webb Ellis, a pupil at the school, who was the first player to pick up and run with the ball during a football game. In 1895, an argument over paying money to players led to a split between rugby clubs in England. Two forms of the sport have existed ever since: the newer, professional (paid) game is known as "Rugby League", which has thirteen players per team, and the more traditional and widely-played amateur (unpaid) version is "Rugby Union", with fifteen players on each side. The rules for each are slightly different, but the basic idea behind both sports remains the same.

TRADITIONAL QUALITY
The company that makes these international match balls was supplying footballs to Rugby school in 1823, when the game was first played there.

GILBERT
MAKER
RUGBY
ENGLAND

Modern leather rugby ball

HUMAN SPIDER
When the teams lock together into a "scrum", they look like a giant spider with many legs. The players in the middle of the scrum are the "hookers" who try and heel the ball backwards for their teammates to pick up.

SKY-SCRAPERS AND SIDE-WINDERS *below*
The tallest Rugby Union goalposts in the world are 33.5 m (110 ft) high. Most players today kick the ball soccer-style, rather than with the toe of the boot, and are known as "side-winders" because of their curved run-up and kicking action.

High-sided rugby boots

WINIT

BOOTING THE BALL *left*
Rugby players may wear soccer shoes or special, high-sided boots which support the ankles. The longest recorded goal-kick was scored in 1932, when the ball was kicked 82 m (270 ft).

MAORI WAR-DANCE
The New Zealand national team is known as the "All Blacks", because of its all-black strip. The first New Zealand touring team consisted mainly of native *maori* players who performed a traditional war-dance, called a "haka", before each game. This is still a feature of matches played by the modern "All Blacks".

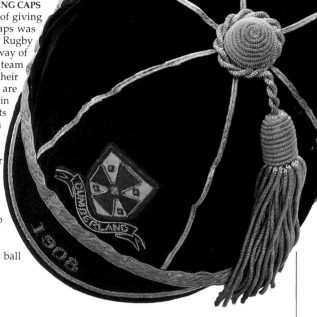

AWARDING CAPS
The practice of giving special caps was introduced at Rugby school as a way of thanking team members for their efforts. Caps are now awarded in other sports too, when players are chosen to play for their country.

1908 Rugby cap

Rounder-style ball made in 1851

THE EVOLUTION OF THE BALL *left*
Early rugby balls were much rounder than they are today. The modern shape makes the ball much easier to carry and throw.

RUNNING WITH THE BALL
One of the most exciting moments in a rugby match is when a player catches the ball and runs the whole length of the field to score a try - hotly pursued by opposing players.

Rugby balls are made from four leather panels, stitched together in the same way as soccer balls (p. 8)

ALTERNATIVE MATERIALS *right*
Over the years, ball-makers have tried making balls out of various materials apart from the traditional leather. Pigskin, and even camelskin, are excellent materials to work with, but balls made from them were found to be too slippery.

Camelskin ball

Hockey

HOCKEY HAS BEEN DESCRIBED in a very simple way as "Association Football [soccer] played with a stick and a cricket-ball in place of a football" and there are, indeed, many ways in which the two sports are alike. Hockey is played by teams of 11 men or women, and is a sport where no physical contact is allowed. Ancient Egyptian and Greek wall-paintings suggest that games like hockey were played as far back as the third century B.C., and the Romans are known to have played a game called *paganica*, that used curved sticks and a leather-covered ball. The modern sport is based on the *hurling*, *bandy* and *shinty* games played in different areas of the British Isles, although the name "hockey" is thought to come from the French word *hoquet*, meaning a "hooked stick".

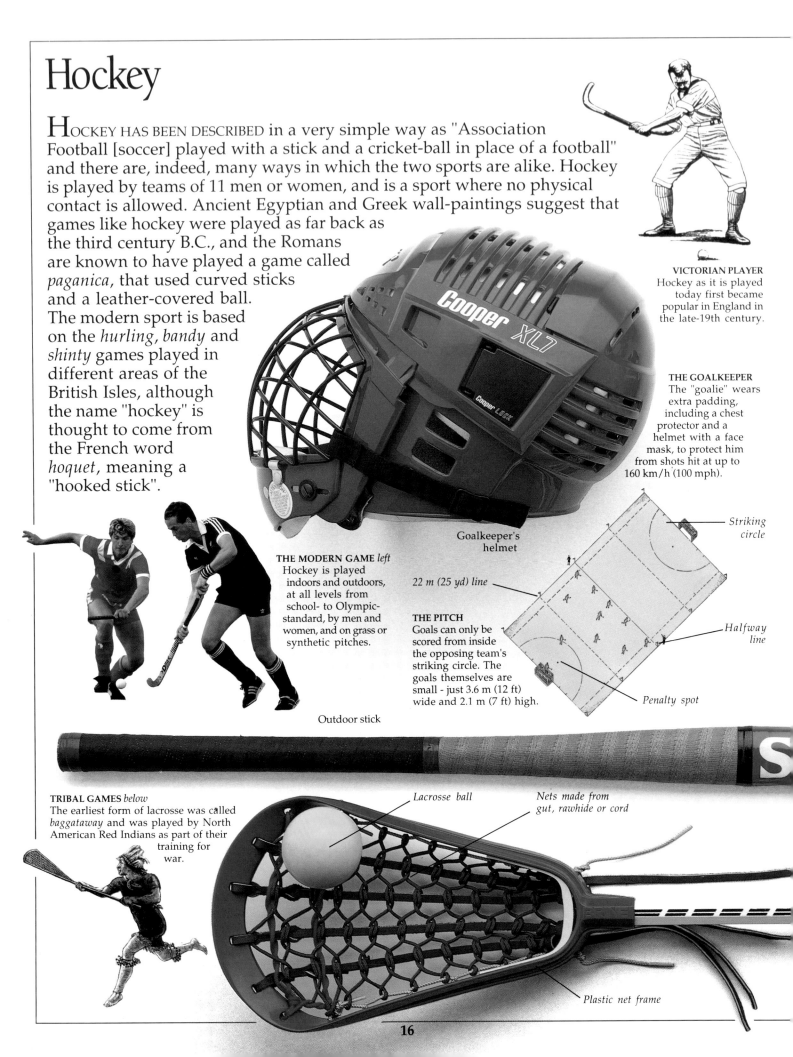

VICTORIAN PLAYER
Hockey as it is played today first became popular in England in the late-19th century.

THE GOALKEEPER
The "goalie" wears extra padding, including a chest protector and a helmet with a face mask, to protect him from shots hit at up to 160 km/h (100 mph).

Goalkeeper's helmet

THE MODERN GAME *left*
Hockey is played indoors and outdoors, at all levels from school- to Olympic-standard, by men and women, and on grass or synthetic pitches.

Outdoor stick

22 m (25 yd) line

THE PITCH
Goals can only be scored from inside the opposing team's striking circle. The goals themselves are small - just 3.6 m (12 ft) wide and 2.1 m (7 ft) high.

Striking circle

Halfway line

Penalty spot

TRIBAL GAMES *below*
The earliest form of lacrosse was called *baggataway* and was played by North American Red Indians as part of their training for war.

Lacrosse ball

Nets made from gut, rawhide or cord

Plastic net frame

KICKERS
The goalkeeper is the only player allowed to touch the ball with his feet. He wears special "kickers" outside his boots, with which he blocks the ball and kicks it clear of his goal.

Rigid palm 5 cm (2 in) thick

Straps fit over normal boots

Padded toes protect feet against the hard ball

FOOTWEAR
The boots worn by hockey players depend on the type of pitch they are playing on. Soccer-style boots are usually worn on grass, and special, multi-studded shoes like these on synthetic pitches.

GAUNTLETS
The 'keeper's gloves are different for each hand. One is flexible, so he can pick the ball up when he has to, and the other has a rigid, padded palm that is used to stop the ball.

Padding extends below the wrist to protect the forearm

Over 60 moulded studs on each sole

STICK HEADS *below*
Sticks have a rounded side and a flat face, with which the ball is struck. No part of the stick is allowed to be more than 5 cm (2 in) wide.

Indoor stick

THE BALL
The hard hockey ball is similar in size to a baseball or cricket ball and is usually white.

TYPES OF STICKS *above*
Most modern sticks are made from ash, with a cane handle. The head is steam-bent so that the grain of the wood follows the bend and strengthens the stick. Indoor sticks are lighter and thinner, and old-fashioned sticks had a longer curve.

A lady player of 1912

Old-fashioned stick

Lacrosse

This sport is similar to hockey, but uses sticks with nets to throw, catch and carry the ball. French settlers in North America gave the sport its name, because the hooked sticks reminded them of a bishop's staff or *crozier* ("la crosse"). Men's and women's games are played differently.

Women's crosses are generally shorter than men's

LACROSSE STICK
Sticks are traditionally made from hickory wood, but many are now made from plastic. The net must be tightly strung, so the ball does not become stuck.

INDIAN CROSSE *right*
The type of stick used by the first players varied according to which tribe they came from. Many were decorated with feathers.

Ice hockey

As its name suggests, ice hockey is basically hockey played on ice, and it originated as the winter version of hockey - played on frozen ponds and lakes. However, there are several other major differences between the modern forms of the two sports: Ice hockey teams have six players who use longer sticks and a hard rubber disc, called a "puck", instead of a ball. Modern ice hockey is usually played indoors, where the temperature of the ice is controlled automatically. The ice is resurfaced between each of the three 20-minute periods.

Ice hockey helmet

A modern player in full kit

SPEEDY SPORT
Ice hockey is the fastest team sport in the world. There is also a great deal of body contact, and the players wear padding to protect them when they crash into the barriers that surround the rink.

Elbow pads

BODY ARMOUR
As well as the items shown here, ice hockey players wear special "shorts" that have thick padding sewn into them to protect the players' legs when they fall on the hard ice. Deliberately tripping an opponent is against the rules, and the offender would be punished by spending time in the "sin bin". These "sentences" vary according to the offence committed, and may be for two, five or ten minutes.

Shoulder and chest padding

GLOVES
The gauntlets worn by outfield players are heavily padded and made from leather or synthetic materials. Rigid fingertip caps provide extra protection. Goaltenders wear a different sort of glove on each hand - a "catcher" and a "blocker".

FROZEN PUCK
The disc-shaped puck is made from toughened ("vulcanized") rubber. It is generally kept frozen before a match so that it keeps its original form as long as possible.

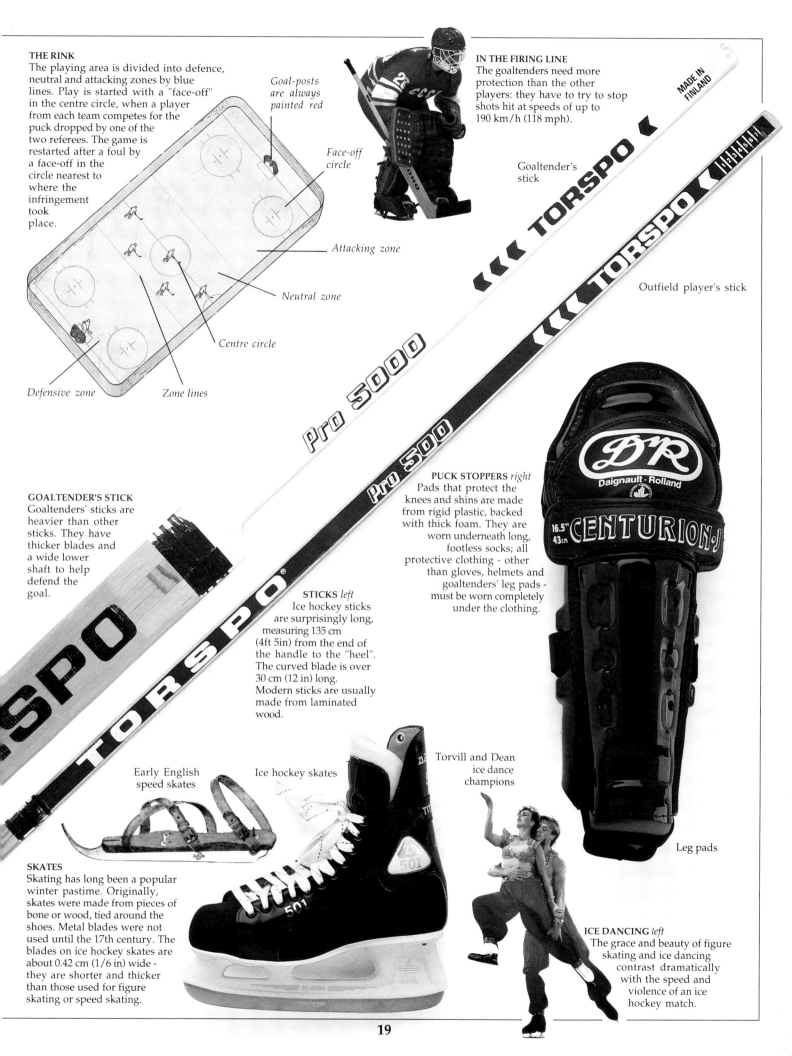

THE RINK
The playing area is divided into defence, neutral and attacking zones by blue lines. Play is started with a "face-off" in the centre circle, when a player from each team competes for the puck dropped by one of the two referees. The game is restarted after a foul by a face-off in the circle nearest to where the infringement took place.

Goal-posts are always painted red

Face-off circle

Attacking zone

Neutral zone

Centre circle

Defensive zone

Zone lines

IN THE FIRING LINE
The goaltenders need more protection than the other players: they have to try to stop shots hit at speeds of up to 190 km/h (118 mph).

Goaltender's stick

MADE IN FINLAND

TORSPO

TORSPO

Pro 5000

Pro 500

TORSPO

TORSPO

Outfield player's stick

GOALTENDER'S STICK
Goaltenders' sticks are heavier than other sticks. They have thicker blades and a wide lower shaft to help defend the goal.

PUCK STOPPERS *right*
Pads that protect the knees and shins are made from rigid plastic, backed with thick foam. They are worn underneath long, footless socks; all protective clothing - other than gloves, helmets and goaltenders' leg pads - must be worn completely under the clothing.

STICKS *left*
Ice hockey sticks are surprisingly long, measuring 135 cm (4ft 5in) from the end of the handle to the "heel". The curved blade is over 30 cm (12 in) long. Modern sticks are usually made from laminated wood.

DR Daignault · Rolland

16.5" 43cm CENTURION·J

Leg pads

Early English speed skates

Ice hockey skates

Torvill and Dean ice dance champions

SKATES
Skating has long been a popular winter pastime. Originally, skates were made from pieces of bone or wood, tied around the shoes. Metal blades were not used until the 17th century. The blades on ice hockey skates are about 0.42 cm (1/6 in) wide - they are shorter and thicker than those used for figure skating or speed skating.

ICE DANCING *left*
The grace and beauty of figure skating and ice dancing contrast dramatically with the speed and violence of an ice hockey match.

19

Basketball

The basketball has a circumference of 75-78 cm (30-31 in)

IN 1891, A CANADIAN clergyman invented the game of basketball when he nailed a peach basket to the balcony at each end of the local gymnasium. The object of the game is to score points by throwing the ball into the "basket" at your opponents' end of the court. Basketball is a non-contact sport, played on an indoor court, in which players throw and bounce the ball, but are not allowed to carry or kick it. Because of the height of the baskets, there are many very tall basketball players - the tallest being 2.45 m (8 ft)!

Harlem Globetrotter

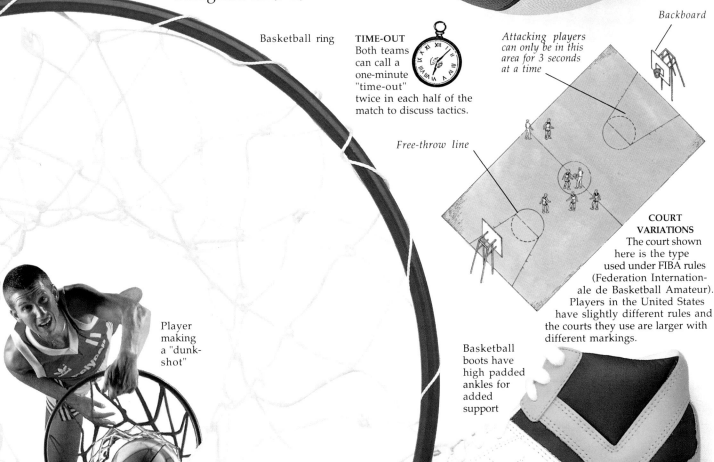

Basketball ring

TIME-OUT
Both teams can call a one-minute "time-out" twice in each half of the match to discuss tactics.

Attacking players can only be in this area for 3 seconds at a time

Backboard

Free-throw line

COURT VARIATIONS
The court shown here is the type used under FIBA rules (Federation International-ale de Basketball Amateur). Players in the United States have slightly different rules and the courts they use are larger with different markings.

Player making a "dunk-shot"

Basketball boots have high padded ankles for added support

CONVERSE®

Netball

Netball is one of the few solely female sports. It is similar to basketball but played on a slightly larger court, with seven players on each side rather than five, and nets supported by poles instead of backboards. Like basketball, it originated in the United States in the second half of the last century.

MOVING WITH THE BALL
Netball players are not allowed to carry the ball. When holding it, the player can turn in any direction, but must keep one of her feet on the same spot.

PLAYING ZONES
Each player is only allowed in certain areas of the court. They wear lettered vests to indicate their positions so the umpire knows if a player is in the wrong zone.

GD WD
C WA
GA GS

Netball

Volleyball

This sport is like a cross between basketball and badminton (p. 35). Teams of six players hit a ball over a net using their hands and arms, or any other part of their upper body. Each team may touch the ball up to three times before it crosses the net.

AT THE NET *left*
The height of the net means that attacking players have to jump high to smash the ball downwards. No player is allowed to touch the net or reach over it into the opposing team's side of the court.

THE BALL *right*
The volleyball is lightweight and of a uniform colour. It is smaller than a netball or basketball.

21

Baseball

THE OFFICIAL NATIONAL SPORT of the United States, baseball is very similar to a number of earlier bat-and-ball games, such as the English game "rounders", which was introduced by the early settlers in the 18th century. The game is divided into nine periods, called "innings", with one team of nine players batting and the other fielding at any one time. The batters have to hit the ball and run between fixed bases to score "runs" for their team, while the fielders try to put the batters "out" by a variety of means - including catching the ball and "tagging" a runner with the ball as he runs between bases. The stars of the sport are those who can hit the ball the furthest, the record being more than 188 m (618 ft).

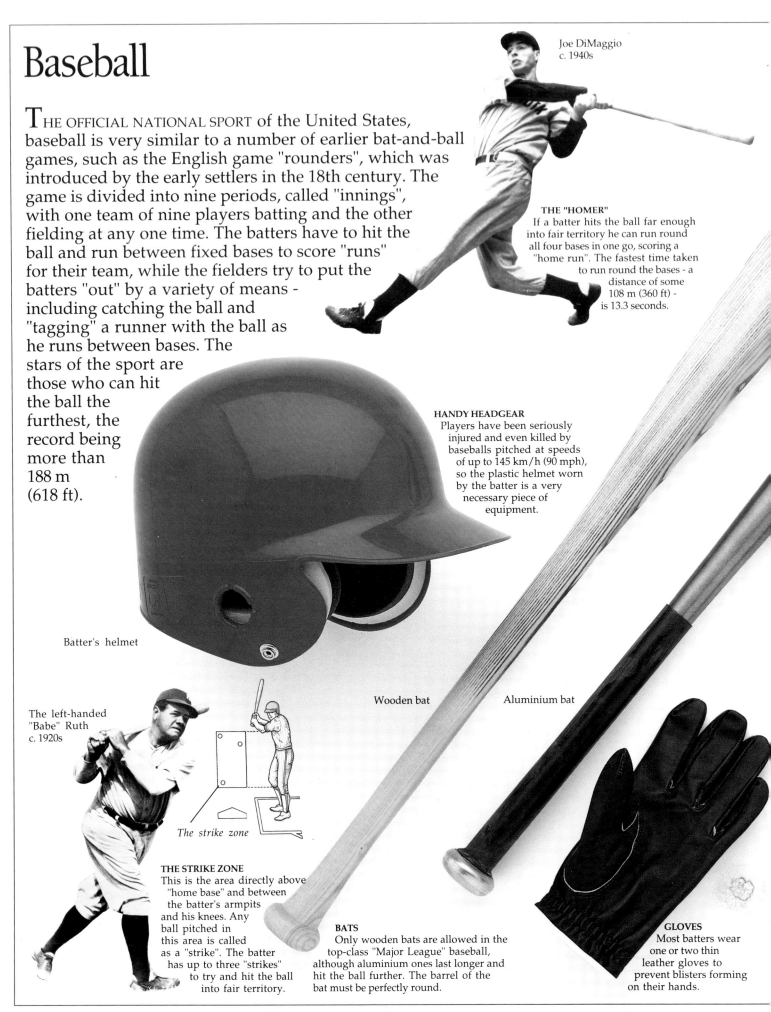

Joe DiMaggio
c. 1940s

THE "HOMER"
If a batter hits the ball far enough into fair territory he can run round all four bases in one go, scoring a "home run". The fastest time taken to run round the bases - a distance of some 108 m (360 ft) - is 13.3 seconds.

HANDY HEADGEAR
Players have been seriously injured and even killed by baseballs pitched at speeds of up to 145 km/h (90 mph), so the plastic helmet worn by the batter is a very necessary piece of equipment.

Batter's helmet

The left-handed "Babe" Ruth c. 1920s

The strike zone

Wooden bat

Aluminium bat

THE STRIKE ZONE
This is the area directly above "home base" and between the batter's armpits and his knees. Any ball pitched in this area is called as a "strike". The batter has up to three "strikes" to try and hit the ball into fair territory.

BATS
Only wooden bats are allowed in the top-class "Major League" baseball, although aluminium ones last longer and hit the ball further. The barrel of the bat must be perfectly round.

GLOVES
Most batters wear one or two thin leather gloves to prevent blisters forming on their hands.

SHIRTS

Shirts must bear no pattern or emblem that could be mistaken for a baseball, nor any shiny glass or polished metal, which could reflect the sun into another player's eyes. Each shirt must have a number at least 15 cm (6 in) high on the back. Some players also wear long-sleeved undershirts.

Baseball

INSIDE THE BALL

The baseball weighs between 142-156 g (5-5.5 oz), and has a very complex structure. Top-quality balls are covered in cowhide or horsehide treated with alum, and are hand-stitched.

Grip for "outcurve" pitch

Red outer stitching

PITCHING

The pitcher must be able to throw fast and slow balls that curve in the air in various directions. The way in which the ball is gripped determines the type of pitch he delivers.

Horsehide strips

Woollen strands

Cork centre

Rubber inner casing

Cotton thread outer casing

Woollen yarn

A baseball pitcher

AN INTERNATIONAL SPORT

Although baseball is primarily an American sport, it is played by enthusiasts in other countries too. The International Baseball Association is the co-ordinating body of the sport around the world.

Foul territory

Outfield

2nd base

3rd base

Infield

Pitcher

Batter

Catcher

Home base

1st base

Umpire

THE "DIAMOND"

The baseball diamond is bordered by the four bases which surround the infield. The area outside this is divided into the outfield and foul territory - into which the ball should not be hit. The home plate and the pitcher's rubber are slabs of white rubber, and the other bases are made from canvas bags filled with soft material.

Baseball pants

PANTS

The tradition-al baseball outfit includes breeches that reach just below the knee. Separate stirrups are worn over the socks.

Stirrups

SLIDING INTO BASE

A batter is forced out if a player with the ball touches first base before he does. At other bases, runners will dive head-first into the base to avoid getting tagged out.

Metal shoe plates

Plastic heel plate

Plastic toe plates

BASEBALL BOOTS

As with other sports, the type of shoes worn depends on whether the surface is natural or synthetic grass. Toe and heel plates are screwed to the sole of boots worn on natural grass; pointed spikes are not allowed.

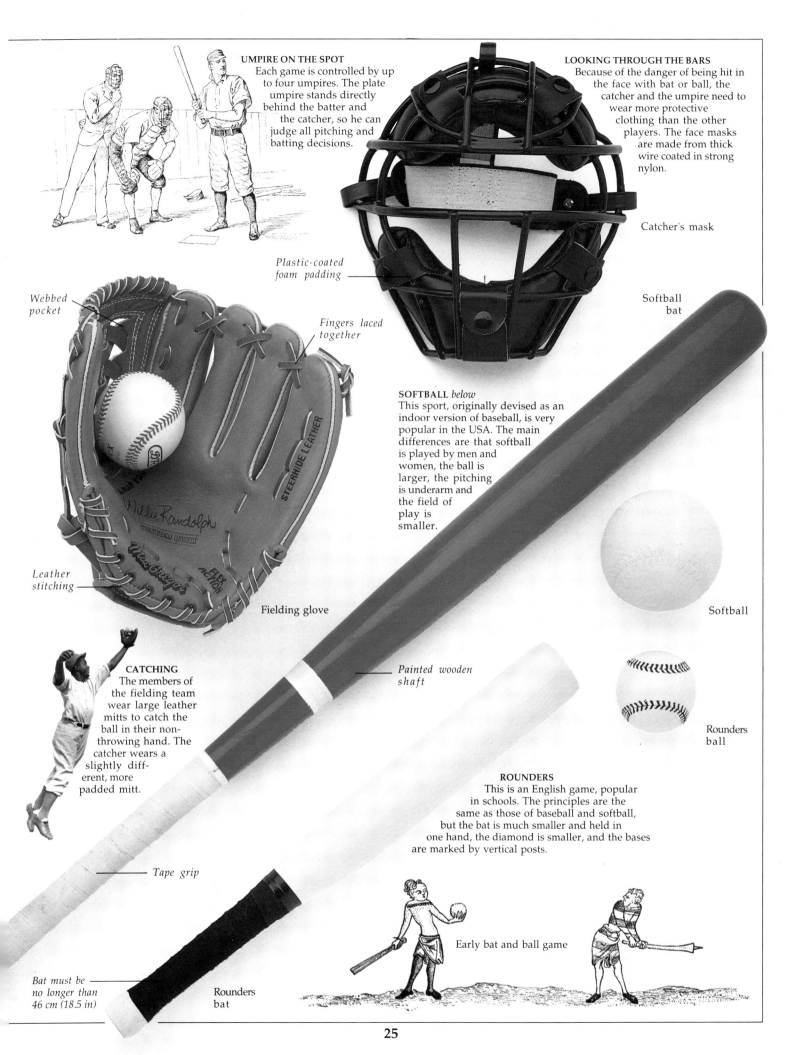

UMPIRE ON THE SPOT
Each game is controlled by up to four umpires. The plate umpire stands directly behind the batter and the catcher, so he can judge all pitching and batting decisions.

LOOKING THROUGH THE BARS
Because of the danger of being hit in the face with bat or ball, the catcher and the umpire need to wear more protective clothing than the other players. The face masks are made from thick wire coated in strong nylon.

Catcher's mask

Plastic-coated foam padding

Webbed pocket

Fingers laced together

Softball bat

SOFTBALL *below*
This sport, originally devised as an indoor version of baseball, is very popular in the USA. The main differences are that softball is played by men and women, the ball is larger, the pitching is underarm and the field of play is smaller.

Leather stitching

Fielding glove

Softball

CATCHING
The members of the fielding team wear large leather mitts to catch the ball in their non-throwing hand. The catcher wears a slightly different, more padded mitt.

Painted wooden shaft

Rounders ball

ROUNDERS
This is an English game, popular in schools. The principles are the same as those of baseball and softball, but the bat is much smaller and held in one hand, the diamond is smaller, and the bases are marked by vertical posts.

Tape grip

Early bat and ball game

Bat must be no longer than 46 cm (18.5 in)

Rounders bat

25

Cricket

CRICKET IS BROADLY SIMILAR to baseball (p. 22), in that teams take it in turns to bat and field. The two sports differ in that there are two cricket batsmen on the field at any one time and they must defend the "wicket" with their bat and score by running between the two wickets at opposite ends of the narrow pitch. Four runs are automatically scored if the ball is hit over the boundary of the field, and six if it crosses the boundary without touching the ground. Bat-and-ball games like cricket were probably played in England as long ago as the 13th century.

A gentleman cricketer

Wicketkeeper — *Wicket*

Batsman

THE PITCH
The cricket pitch is a narrow strip of close-mown grass, 20 m (66 ft) long, with a wicket at each end. "Overs" (sequences of six balls) are bowled from alternate ends.

Bowler
Umpire
Bowling crease

Replica of an 18th-century bat

Screw-in spikes

BOOTS
Many cricketers prefer to wear high-sided boots with screw-in metal spikes. Traditionally, cricket clothing and footwear is mainly white or off-white in colour.

Wicketkeeper's gloves

Pimpled rubber

AN EARLY GAME
Cricket in the 18th century was played with five players in each team. There was only one wicket, and this had two stumps, rather than three.

BOWLING
Cricketers bowl over-arm, so the ball bounces once before reaching the batsman. Slow bowlers spin the ball with their fingers, so that it turns towards or away from the batsman, and faster bowlers bounce the ball off its raised seam to get a similar effect.

THE BALL
The cricket ball is made in a similar way to a baseball (p. 23), but is covered with red leather and has a straight stitched seam.

Bails

Stumps

THE WICKETKEEPER
The wicketkeeper plays a similar role to the catcher in baseball (p. 21). Like the catcher, he wears leg guards because he is so close to the batsman. His well-padded gloves have pimpled-rubber palms to help grip the ball.

THE FIRST BATS
The word "cricket" may come from *cric*, the old English term for a shepherd's crook, which the early cricket bats resembled. 18th-century bats were long and heavy with a curved blade. The modern style of straight bat was not used until the introduction of over-arm bowling.

WICKETS
Arguments about whether or not the ball had passed between the two stumps were so common that a middle stump was introduced. Modern wickets are made from ash, and are 71 cm (28 in) high.

BATTING GLOVES
These protect the fingers from injury but allow enough freedom of movement to grip and wield the bat.

The weather vane depicting Old Father Time is a famous Lord's landmark

HAT-TRICK *right*
Early cricketers wore top hats which were also presented to bowlers who took three wickets in a row - hence the term "hat-trick".

Modern cricket helmet

Protective plastic ear pieces

THE HOME OF CRICKET
Lord's cricket ground, known as the "home of cricket", was founded by Thomas Lord in 1787, and is the headquarters of the M.C.C. (Marylebone Cricket Club) who drew up the rules of the game. International matches are often played at Lord's; these last for five days and are known as "test" matches. The bat shown here has been signed by players taking part in a test match at Lord's.

COLOURED CLOTHES
In floodlit cricket matches, each team wears a different-coloured strip. A white ball is used as it can be seen more easily.

Fastening straps

METAL BAT
An aluminium bat was used by a few players during the 1970s, but the fashion did not last long as it proved no substitute for the traditional wooden variety.

Metal bats had a hollow construction

A MODERN BAT
Today's cricket bats are made from willow and have a cane handle, usually covered by a rubber grip. The average bat weighs about 1050 g (2lb 5oz), and is roughly half the weight of the old bat shown opposite.

LEG PADS *right*
These protect the shins of the batsmen and wicketkeeper. The pads reach to the thigh, but still allow the batsman to run between the wickets. Batsmen can be "out" if they use their legs to stop the ball hitting the wicket.

Ankle padding

27

How cricket bats are made

The introduction of fast over-arm bowling in the early-19th century meant that batsmen needed lighter bats that could be wielded more easily. The modern type of bat dates from that time and, despite various improvements in design, the style of the bat has changed little since then. The bat blade, which absorbs the impact of the ball, is made from willow, while the springy cane-and-rubber handle protects the hands from the shock of striking the ball.

THE TREE
Of the 36 varieties of English willow, only *Salix coerulea* and *S. virida* are suitable to be made into top-quality cricket bats. These are lightweight woods with a very straight grain.

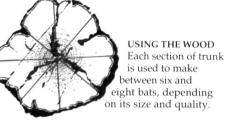

USING THE WOOD
Each section of trunk is used to make between six and eight bats, depending on its size and quality.

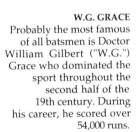

W.G. GRACE
Probably the most famous of all batsmen is Doctor William Gilbert ("W.G.") Grace who dominated the sport throughout the second half of the 19th century. During his career, he scored over 54,000 runs.

Rubber *Cane*

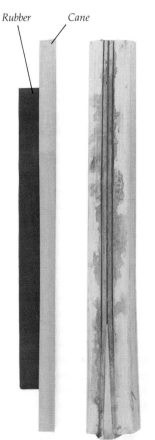

Twine wrapped around handle

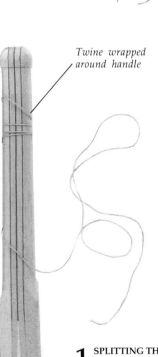

THE HANDLE
The handle is made from pieces of *Sarawak* cane, formed into blocks with strips of rubber, and bonded together tightly with strong animal glue.

1 SPLITTING THE TRUNK
Each 70 cm (28 in) length of willow trunk is cut into segments or "clefts", then the bark is removed. The young outer "sapwood" is best for making bats; it is a lighter colour than the inner "heartwood".

Sapwood

2 THE SEASONING PROCESS
The clefts are sawn into "blades", stacked and left to dry for 2-4 weeks. Then they are put into a kiln to dry for a further 4-6 weeks.

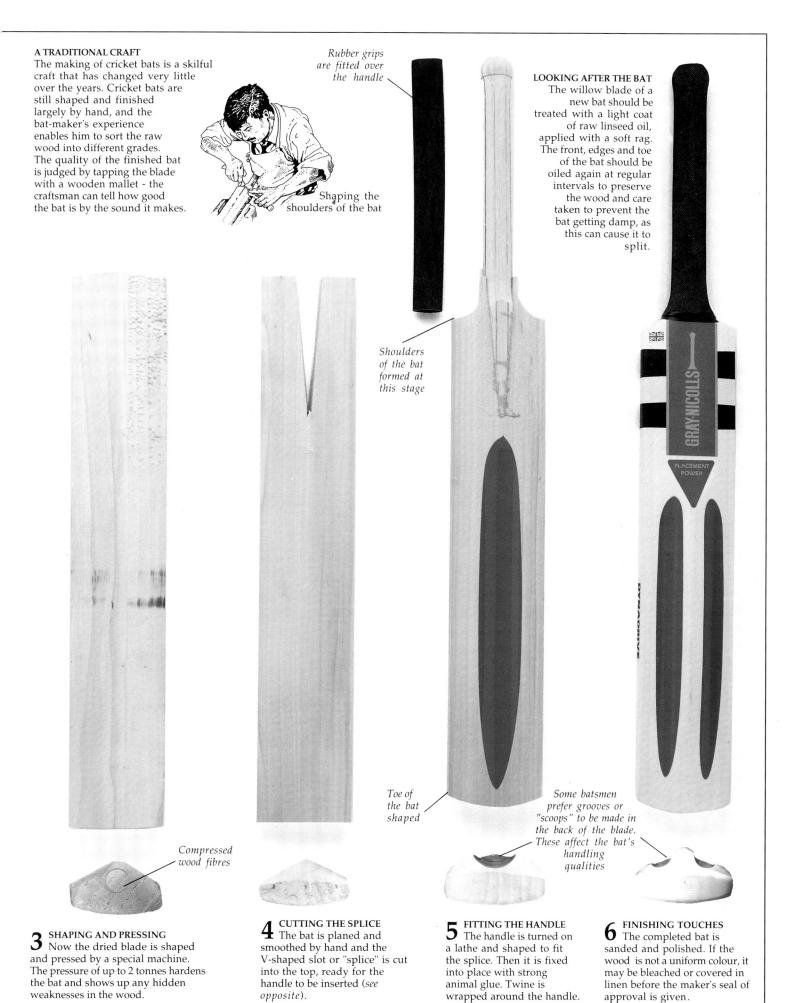

A TRADITIONAL CRAFT
The making of cricket bats is a skilful craft that has changed very little over the years. Cricket bats are still shaped and finished largely by hand, and the bat-maker's experience enables him to sort the raw wood into different grades. The quality of the finished bat is judged by tapping the blade with a wooden mallet - the craftsman can tell how good the bat is by the sound it makes.

Rubber grips are fitted over the handle

Shaping the shoulders of the bat

LOOKING AFTER THE BAT
The willow blade of a new bat should be treated with a light coat of raw linseed oil, applied with a soft rag. The front, edges and toe of the bat should be oiled again at regular intervals to preserve the wood and care taken to prevent the bat getting damp, as this can cause it to split.

Shoulders of the bat formed at this stage

Toe of the bat shaped

Some batsmen prefer grooves or "scoops" to be made in the back of the blade. These affect the bat's handling qualities

Compressed wood fibres

3 SHAPING AND PRESSING
Now the dried blade is shaped and pressed by a special machine. The pressure of up to 2 tonnes hardens the bat and shows up any hidden weaknesses in the wood.

4 CUTTING THE SPLICE
The bat is planed and smoothed by hand and the V-shaped slot or "splice" is cut into the top, ready for the handle to be inserted (*see opposite*).

5 FITTING THE HANDLE
The handle is turned on a lathe and shaped to fit the splice. Then it is fixed into place with strong animal glue. Twine is wrapped around the handle.

6 FINISHING TOUCHES
The completed bat is sanded and polished. If the wood is not a uniform colour, it may be bleached or covered in linen before the maker's seal of approval is given.

Tennis

TENNIS IS PLAYED by two or four people on a court divided by a low net. Each player has a racket and points are scored by hitting a ball over the net in such a way that it bounces inside the court and cannot be returned. "Real", or Royal, tennis originated in France during the Middle Ages, and was very popular among the European noblemen of the 16th century, but it was not until the 19th century that "lawn tennis" was first played. The sport quickly became very popular with both men and women. Today, tennis is played on clay, cement, wood and plastic courts, as well as on grass.

Wooden frame

Angled racket head

Natural gut strings

REAL TENNIS
Real - or Royal - tennis used to be the sport of kings, and was a favourite pastime of the French and English monarchy. Henry VIII of England built a court at his Hampton Court palace in the 16th century, and this is still used by real tennis enthusiasts today.

An old-fashioned scoreboard

Sideline (doubles)

Net

Sideline (singles)

Baseline

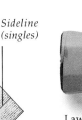

Service court

The tennis court

GAME, SET AND MATCH
Opposing players serve alternate games. At least six games must be won to gain a set, and two - or sometimes three - sets are needed to win a match. Up to eleven officials, not including the umpire, are needed at top matches. They sit around the edge of the court and judge whether the ball is "in" or "out".

Grip

Lawn tennis racket

A STICKY START
Tennis first became popular in the 1870s when it was known as *sphairistike* - the Greek word for "ball-game". This was soon shortened to "sticky".

Hevea brasiliensis rubber tree

The tennis ball

The progression from real tennis, played on indoor courts, to lawn tennis, played in the gardens of "polite society," was not as obvious as it may seem. Indeed, before it was possible at all, somebody had to invent a ball that would bounce on grass!

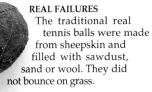

REAL FAILURES
The traditional real tennis balls were made from sheepskin and filled with sawdust, sand or wool. They did not bounce on grass.

RAW RUBBER
Latex (rubber) comes from the stems of certain trees. It was not until the 19th century that rubber-tree seeds were brought to Europe and grown commercially.

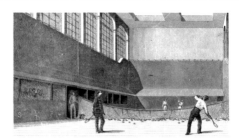

CLOISTER COURT
Real tennis courts have gallery "rooves" jutting out around three of the four sides, and points are won according to how the ball is hit into and through the galleries. The strange design of the court is like the monastery cloisters where the game was first played.

IN THE CHAIR
The tennis umpire sits in a high chair next to the net, so he has the best possible view of the match. He announces the score after each point has been played.

Real tennis racket

WIMBLEDON
The oldest and most important tennis championships are held at the All England Tennis and Croquet Club, Wimbledon, London. The first championships were held in 1877.

Moulded graphite frame

PUMA HI-FLECK GRAPHITE

UNIVERSAL MIDSIZE

GRAPHITE · COMPOSITE

Throat

Synthetic strings

SPACE-AGE RACKET
The modern tennis racket is stronger and more powerful than ever before. Computers are used to help design the rackets, which are made from materials developed for the aerospace industry.

Head

HOW THE BALL IS MADE
The rubber is "vulcanized" (treated with sulphur at high temperatures) to make it stronger and more elastic. The hollow ball is formed from two halves bonded together.

THE COVERING
The plain rubber ball was rather slippery in wet conditions, so a flannel covering was invented. Modern balls are covered with a mixture of wool and man-made fibres.

Wilson 2

BALL CHANGES
The pressure inside the ball changes in different conditions and during play, so the balls used in major matches are kept refrigerated at 20°C (68°F), and replaced after every few games.

Wilson 2

Tennis rackets

The sport we know today as tennis can be traced back to the French game of *Jeu de Paume*, in which two players hit a ball to each other with the palm of their hand. Soon, pieces of wood and webbed gloves started to be used instead and, by the start of the 15th century, strung "rackets" had been invented. Today's rackets are the result of trial-and-error over the years; until very recently, there were no rules governing the design and proportions of the racket, and many different styles and materials have been used during the past 100 years. Different kinds of stringing have also been tried - even wire "strings" were used at one stage.

International Tennis Federation rules now state that the overall dimensions of any racket must not exceed 81.28 cm (32 in) in length and 31.75 cm (12.5 in) in width, and that there must only be one set of strings on each racket.

Lady player of 1890

Aluminium frame

Piano wire strings

Solid ash frame

1900s *below*
By the early years of the 20th century, the familiar symmetrical shape of the racket had been introduced. A popular feature of the period was the "fishtail" handle - considered to be the height of fashion. Grooves were often cut into the handle to improve the grip.

FIRST METAL RACKET *right*
During the 1920s, experimental rackets with aluminium frames were made. The fact that they were strung with piano wire did nothing for their appeal, as it meant that the wool-covered tennis balls quickly wore out.

1920s *above*
Leather grips were introduced around this time to make the racket much easier to hold. Most racket frames were still being made from a solid piece of ash, but the shafts were becoming narrower and the edges more rounded to reduce wind resistance.

Leather grip

Symmetrical head

Fishtail handle

Grooved grip

1880s *below*
The first lawn-tennis rackets were similar to those used in real tennis, with off-set, pear-shaped heads. They weighed much the same as modern rackets but the natural gut was much coarser and strung more loosely than today.

Plain wooden handle

Off-set head

1930s *below*
The "Hazell's Streamline" racket has an unusual handle, designed to reduce wind resistance, and a "laminated" head. Using several thin layers of different woods, rather than a solid piece, means the racket is lighter, stronger and cheaper to make.

Forehand ground stroke

Backhand volley

Serve

Laminated frame

USING THE RACKET
To achieve the maximum control over each stroke, the racket must travel exactly along the direction and height the player wishes the ball to go, but the racket is used in a different way for each type of shot. Ground strokes involve "swinging" the racket, whereas the volley needs a "punching" technique; the serving action is one of "throwing" the racket at the ball, and the lob is a "scooping" stroke.

Forehand lob

Reinforced shoulders

Streamlined handle to reduce wind resistance

Double stringing

1950s *above*
This classic wooden racket was the most popular design for two decades. The frame has multiple laminations of ash and other woods that are used for decoration and to make the racket stronger. The "shoulders" are reinforced for added strength.

Narrow aluminium frame

Moulded graphite frame

1970s *above*
This decade saw the appearance of improved metal rackets. These could be made with a narrower frame than wooden rackets of the same strength, which meant they could travel faster through the air. Some rackets were double-strung to give extra spin to the ball, but this style of stringing has now been banned.

1980s *above*
Nowadays, no top-class players use wooden rackets and very few use metal ones. Instead, racket frames are moulded from a combination of materials such as carbon graphite, fibreglass, boron and ceramic.

Table tennis and badminton

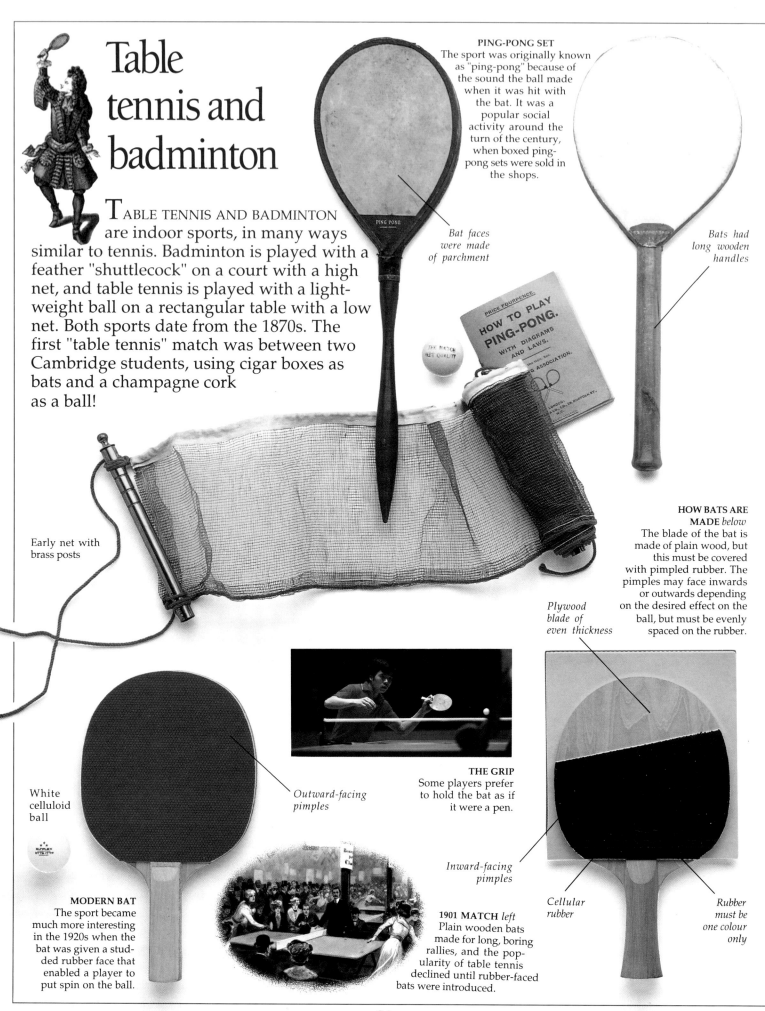

TABLE TENNIS AND BADMINTON are indoor sports, in many ways similar to tennis. Badminton is played with a feather "shuttlecock" on a court with a high net, and table tennis is played with a lightweight ball on a rectangular table with a low net. Both sports date from the 1870s. The first "table tennis" match was between two Cambridge students, using cigar boxes as bats and a champagne cork as a ball!

PING-PONG SET
The sport was originally known as "ping-pong" because of the sound the ball made when it was hit with the bat. It was a popular social activity around the turn of the century, when boxed ping-pong sets were sold in the shops.

Bat faces were made of parchment

Bats had long wooden handles

PRICE FOURPENCE.
HOW TO PLAY PING-PONG.
WITH DIAGRAMS AND LAWS.

Early net with brass posts

HOW BATS ARE MADE *below*
The blade of the bat is made of plain wood, but this must be covered with pimpled rubber. The pimples may face inwards or outwards depending on the desired effect on the ball, but must be evenly spaced on the rubber.

Plywood blade of even thickness

Outward-facing pimples

White celluloid ball

THE GRIP
Some players prefer to hold the bat as if it were a pen.

Inward-facing pimples

Cellular rubber

Rubber must be one colour only

MODERN BAT
The sport became much more interesting in the 1920s when the bat was given a studded rubber face that enabled a player to put spin on the ball.

1901 MATCH *left*
Plain wooden bats made for long, boring rallies, and the popularity of table tennis declined until rubber-faced bats were introduced.

Badminton

Question: which international sport is named after somebody's house? Answer - Badminton; called after the ancestral home of the Duke of Beaufort in Gloucestershire, England. The sport is thought to have been adapted from a children's game as an after-dinner entertainment for the Duke's guests.

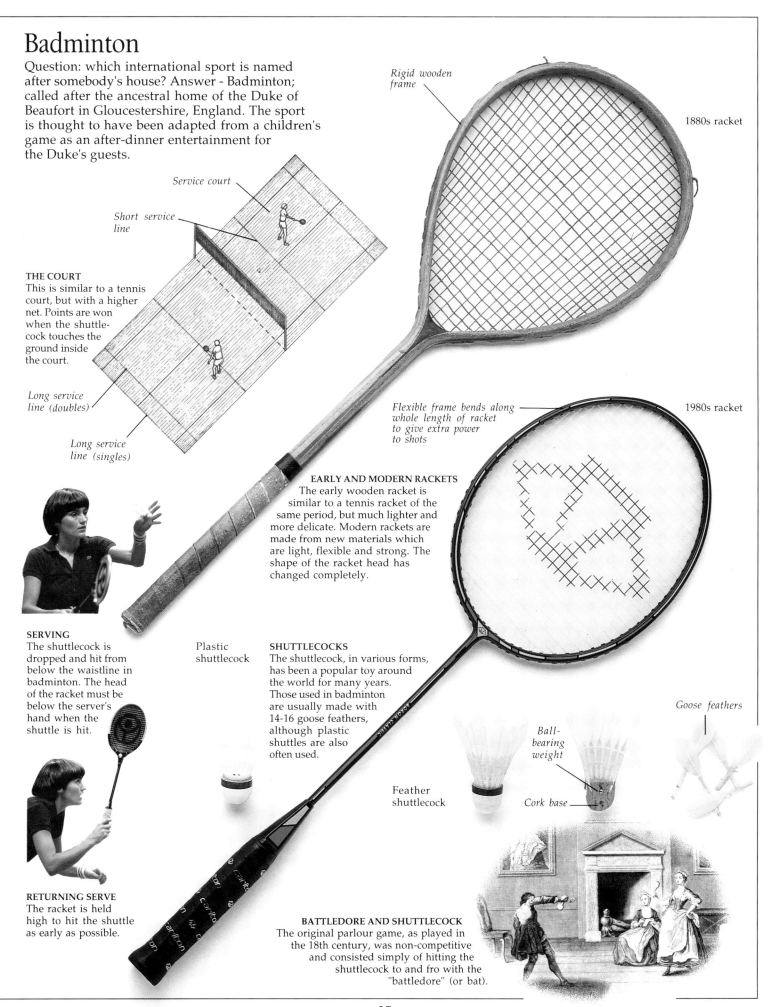

Service court

Short service line

THE COURT
This is similar to a tennis court, but with a higher net. Points are won when the shuttle-cock touches the ground inside the court.

Long service line (doubles)

Long service line (singles)

Rigid wooden frame

1880s racket

Flexible frame bends along whole length of racket to give extra power to shots

1980s racket

EARLY AND MODERN RACKETS
The early wooden racket is similar to a tennis racket of the same period, but much lighter and more delicate. Modern rackets are made from new materials which are light, flexible and strong. The shape of the racket head has changed completely.

SERVING
The shuttlecock is dropped and hit from below the waistline in badminton. The head of the racket must be below the server's hand when the shuttle is hit.

Plastic shuttlecock

SHUTTLECOCKS
The shuttlecock, in various forms, has been a popular toy around the world for many years. Those used in badminton are usually made with 14-16 goose feathers, although plastic shuttles are also often used.

Goose feathers

Ball-bearing weight

Feather shuttlecock

Cork base

RETURNING SERVE
The racket is held high to hit the shuttle as early as possible.

BATTLEDORE AND SHUTTLECOCK
The original parlour game, as played in the 18th century, was non-competitive and consisted simply of hitting the shuttlecock to and fro with the "battledore" (or bat).

Squash and racketball

SQUASH, OR "SQUASH RACKETS", is one of several sports played on a court with four walls; others include rackets, fives, paddleball, racketball and court handball. One player hits the ball against the front wall and the other tries to return it before it has bounced more than once on the floor. The old game of rackets was first played in the 18th century in Fleet Prison, London; the inmates took to hitting a ball against the prison walls as a way of passing the time. A hundred years later, rackets players at Harrow school invented squash as a practice game, its name coming from the soft or "squashy" ball that was used. Like the other racket sports, squash and racketball can be played by two (singles) or four players (doubles). In America, squash is played on a narrower court and with a much harder (almost solid) ball.

| Yellow dot (very slow) | White dot (slow) | Red dot (fast) | Blue dot (very fast) |

Protective strip prevents damage to the racket head

Each racket has about 8.2 m (27 ft) of string

COLOUR-CODED BALLS
Temperature and other weather conditions affect the performance of the hollow rubber ball. Squash balls are made in four varieties - ranging from very slow, for hot conditions, to very fast for cold conditions. The different kinds of ball are coded with coloured dots. Most top players use the very slow ball, which has a less pronounced bounce.

THE RACKET
Squash rackets have a smaller, rounder head than those used for badminton or tennis. Like other rackets, most modern squash rackets are now made from materials such as carbon graphite and fibreglass. Some rackets have a frame with a hollow core that reduces racket vibration when the ball is hit.

Squash racket

Synthetic strings

Natural gut strings

STRINGS
For all racket sports, the choice of strings is very important as the string is the only part of the racket that actually touches the ball. Nowadays, synthetic strings are popular with many players; each string may have up to 48 individual plastic strands, or "filaments", and many are coated with silicone and nylon to protect them from dirt and moisture. Natural gut strings are still widely used, too - these are more "elastic" than synthetic strings, so they are strung less tightly on the racket.

Squash court with perspex walls

SPECTATOR SPORT
The development of glass and perspex walls meant that an audience could watch a match from all sides of the court. This made squash much more popular as a spectator sport.

EYE PROTECTORS
Some players wear special shatterproof goggles to protect their eyes in case they are struck by the fast-moving ball.

Racketball

This very modern relative of squash was first played in the United States during the early 1950s. It evolved from court handball and, more directly, from "paddleball" - in which players used wooden bats, or "paddles", rather than strung rackets. As with squash and badminton, points can only be won when a player is serving. When the server loses a rally, his opponent earns the right to serve. The winner is the first player to score 21 points.

Racketball racket

THE BALL
The hollow rubber ball is larger than a squash ball. When dropped from a height of 2.5 m (100 in), it must bounce 1.7-1.8 m (68-72 in) in a temperature of 24.5°C (76°F).

THE RACKET
The racket has a slightly larger head than a squash racket, but the handle is very much shorter. Some players use a wrist thong attached to the end of the handle.

Racketball glove

FAST AND FURIOUS
Squash and racketball are two of the fastest and most energetic of all sports. Good players must be very fit and agile. Players must be ready to play within 10 seconds of the end of the previous rally, and are penalized if they try to delay the game longer in order to regain their strength.

Wrist thong

LEATHER GLOVE
Players may wear a glove on their racket hand to get a better grip on the handle. The sheepskin used for this glove has been treated to make it "tacky".

Squash/racketball shoe

INSIDE A SHOE
Modern sports shoes of all kinds are designed to be strong, light and comfortable. Shoes worn by racket-sports players have to be well padded to avoid jarring the heels and ankles, and ventilated to allow the feet to "breathe".

Padded foam tongue for comfort

PELOTA
This sport, which comes from northern Spain, is played on a long, narrow court by players holding curved baskets, or *cestas*, made from woven reed and attached to a leather glove.

Basque pelota player

Reinforced heel gives support

Rubber soles provide sure grip

Thick sole absorbs shock

Athletics

THE VARIOUS SPORTS that make up athletics are divided into two main groups: track events (running and walking) and field events (jumping and throwing). These are among the earliest and most basic forms of testing speed, strength, agility and stamina, and can be traced back directly to the ancient Greek games, some 4000 years ago. Most athletes only do one or two events, but a few choose to compete in a range of track and field events, the *heptathlon* for women (seven events held over two days) and the *decathlon* for men (ten events over two days).

Hollow relay batons

TEAM EVENT
The relay is the only athletics event in which teams compete directly against each other. A baton is passed between four team members, who each run either 100 m or 400 m.

Starting pistol

"Blanks"

Track events

Races of up to one lap in length are run in eight "lanes". Because the distance around the outside of the track is greater than the inside, the athletes start in a staggered line, so that each one runs an equal distance.

FROM START TO FINISH
Races are started by firing a starting pistol. In top-class meetings, this triggers a highly accurate electronic timing device; ordinary stopwatches are used in lower levels of competition. The athlete is judged to have finished the race when his torso crosses the line (not his arms, legs, head or neck).

1500 m start

5000 m start

200 m start

Staggered starts

Lanes

100 m start

400 m start

Finishing line (all races)

Stopwatch

Olympic torch-bearer

THE OLYMPIC GAMES
The Olympics are held every four years, and include a great variety of different sports, as well as athletics. The Olympic symbol of five interlocking circles represents the five continents of the world.

The Olympic symbol

ON THE BLOCKS *left*
Sprinters use starting blocks that are fixed to the track. They provide a firm base for the foot to push against at the start of the race. Blocks can be connected to a device that detects any false starts - when an athlete's foot leaves the blocks before the gun goes off.

CROSS-COUNTRY RUNNING
As well as track events, there are long-distance races run on roads and across country. Such courses may include obstacles like fences, ditches and streams.

ROAD RUNNING SHOES
Road runners' feet undergo an enormous amount of stress during each race, so their shoes must give support and be very comfortable.

Screw-in spikes

Air-cushioned sole

QUICK MARCH
Walkers differ from runners in that they must have at least a part of one foot in contact with the ground at all times. Walking races are usually over longer distances than running races.

Track shoes

TRACK SHOES *above*
Athletes who race on the track use tight-fitting, lightweight shoes with spiked soles. The spikes provide the best grip on the track and allow sprinters to reach speeds of up to 40 km/h (25 mph).

Starting blocks

HURDLING *left*
As well as "flat" running races, there are those in which the athletes have to jump barriers. Hurdles, used in races up to 400 m, can be knocked over without injuring the runner. The longer-distance event, the "steeplechase", has solid barriers and a water-jump.

Rubber granules

TYPES OF TRACK
Older tracks are made from grass or cinders, but modern tracks are made from synthetic rubber and polyurethane materials, and are used for training and racing in all weathers.

Cross-section of synthetic track

The springy texture of a synthetic track means that athletes can run faster than on other surfaces

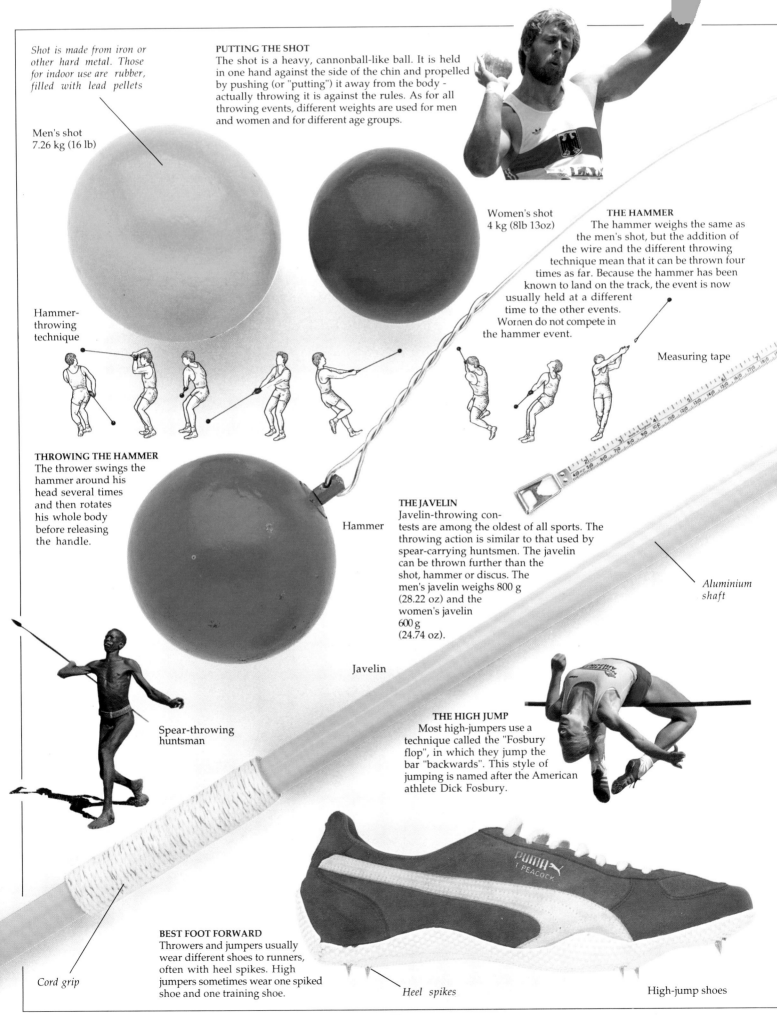

Shot is made from iron or other hard metal. Those for indoor use are rubber, filled with lead pellets

PUTTING THE SHOT

The shot is a heavy, cannonball-like ball. It is held in one hand against the side of the chin and propelled by pushing (or "putting") it away from the body - actually throwing it is against the rules. As for all throwing events, different weights are used for men and women and for different age groups.

Men's shot
7.26 kg (16 lb)

Women's shot
4 kg (8lb 13oz)

THE HAMMER

The hammer weighs the same as the men's shot, but the addition of the wire and the different throwing technique mean that it can be thrown four times as far. Because the hammer has been known to land on the track, the event is now usually held at a different time to the other events. Women do not compete in the hammer event.

Hammer-throwing technique

Measuring tape

THROWING THE HAMMER

The thrower swings the hammer around his head several times and then rotates his whole body before releasing the handle.

Hammer

THE JAVELIN

Javelin-throwing contests are among the oldest of all sports. The throwing action is similar to that used by spear-carrying huntsmen. The javelin can be thrown further than the shot, hammer or discus. The men's javelin weighs 800 g (28.22 oz) and the women's javelin 600 g (24.74 oz).

Aluminium shaft

Javelin

Spear-throwing huntsman

THE HIGH JUMP

Most high-jumpers use a technique called the "Fosbury flop", in which they jump the bar "backwards". This style of jumping is named after the American athlete Dick Fosbury.

BEST FOOT FORWARD

Throwers and jumpers usually wear different shoes to runners, often with heel spikes. High jumpers sometimes wear one spiked shoe and one training shoe.

Cord grip

Heel spikes

High-jump shoes

Field events

The field events take place in the area enclosed by the track, although the runways for the long jump, triple jump and pole vault are sometimes situated outside the track. The hammer and discus are thrown from inside a wire safety cage to protect spectators from wayward throws.

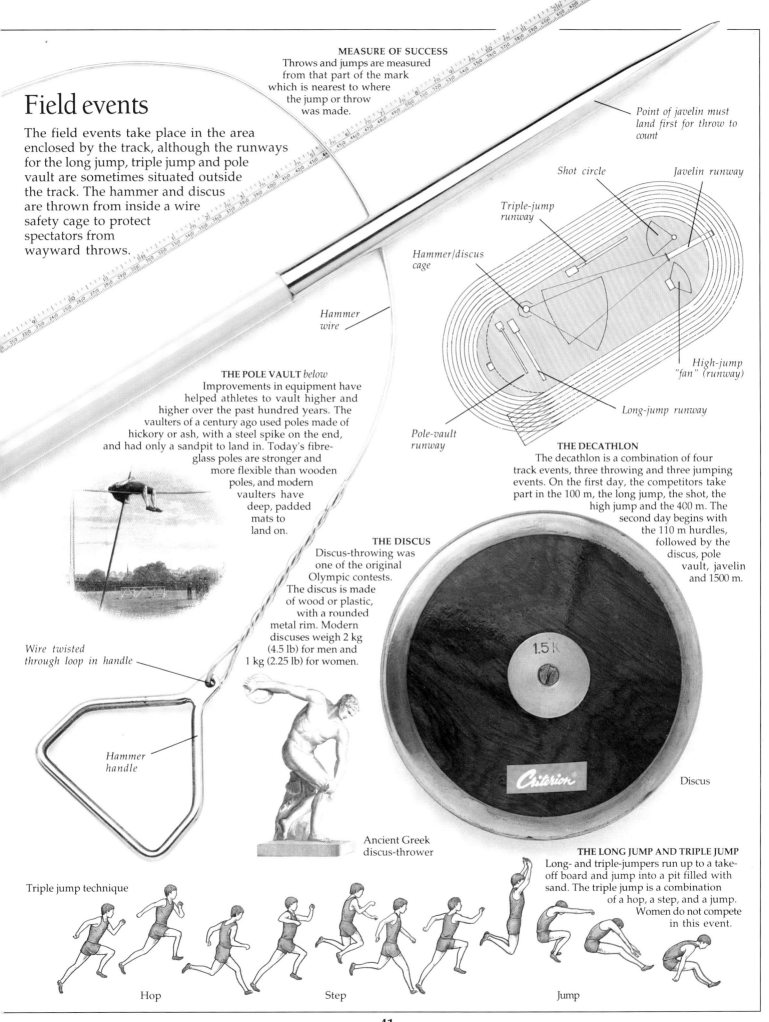

MEASURE OF SUCCESS
Throws and jumps are measured from that part of the mark which is nearest to where the jump or throw was made.

Point of javelin must land first for throw to count

Shot circle

Javelin runway

Triple-jump runway

Hammer/discus cage

Hammer wire

High-jump "fan" (runway)

Long-jump runway

Pole-vault runway

THE POLE VAULT *below*
Improvements in equipment have helped athletes to vault higher and higher over the past hundred years. The vaulters of a century ago used poles made of hickory or ash, with a steel spike on the end, and had only a sandpit to land in. Today's fibre-glass poles are stronger and more flexible than wooden poles, and modern vaulters have deep, padded mats to land on.

THE DECATHLON
The decathlon is a combination of four track events, three throwing and three jumping events. On the first day, the competitors take part in the 100 m, the long jump, the shot, the high jump and the 400 m. The second day begins with the 110 m hurdles, followed by the discus, pole vault, javelin and 1500 m.

THE DISCUS
Discus-throwing was one of the original Olympic contests. The discus is made of wood or plastic, with a rounded metal rim. Modern discuses weigh 2 kg (4.5 lb) for men and 1 kg (2.25 lb) for women.

1.5 K

Criterion

Discus

Wire twisted through loop in handle

Hammer handle

Ancient Greek discus-thrower

THE LONG JUMP AND TRIPLE JUMP
Long- and triple-jumpers run up to a take-off board and jump into a pit filled with sand. The triple jump is a combination of a hop, a step, and a jump. Women do not compete in this event.

Triple jump technique

Hop

Step

Jump

Gymnastics

GYMNASTICS IS A MIXTURE of different events, testing strength, agility, co-ordination and balance. Gymnasts use standard pieces of apparatus on which they perform a series of exercises that are marked by judges. Men compete in six events: the rings, pommel horse, parallel bars, high bar, vault and floor exercises. Women also compete in the vault and floor exercises, as well as on the beam and assymetric bars. A modern gymnasium can have many other kinds of equipment that people can use to "keep fit".

RIBBON RHYTHM
The floor exercises are performed on a marked-out area 12 m (40 ft) square. Gymnasts must make use of this whole area, but are not allowed to step outside it. The exercises consist of tumbling, jumping and balancing movements; ladies' floor exercises may be accompanied by music. A recent variation on the sport is "rhythmic" gymnastics, in which female gymnasts perform floor exercises with ribbons, balls, hoops, ropes and Indian clubs.

PARALLEL BARS *below*
Movements performed on the parallel bars have names such as "peach basket" and "elephant lift". The record number of parallel bar "dips" (push-ups) is over 700 in a 30-minute period.

HANGING AROUND
The rings are suspended 2.5 m (8ft 4in) from the ground. All the movements must be performed without making the rings swing back and forth on their frame.

Wooden rings are 18 cm (7 in) in diameter

WALKING THE PLANK
Gymnasts do somersaults, cartwheels and turns on the beam, which is 5 m (16.5 ft) long and 120 cm (4 ft) off the ground. Performing on the beam is a real balancing act as it is only 10 cm (4 in) wide.

HIGH BAR
Exercises on the high bar must consist of non-stop swinging movements, with backward and forward swings and changes of grip. As with other events, the high bar is judged according to how difficult the exercises are and how well they are performed.

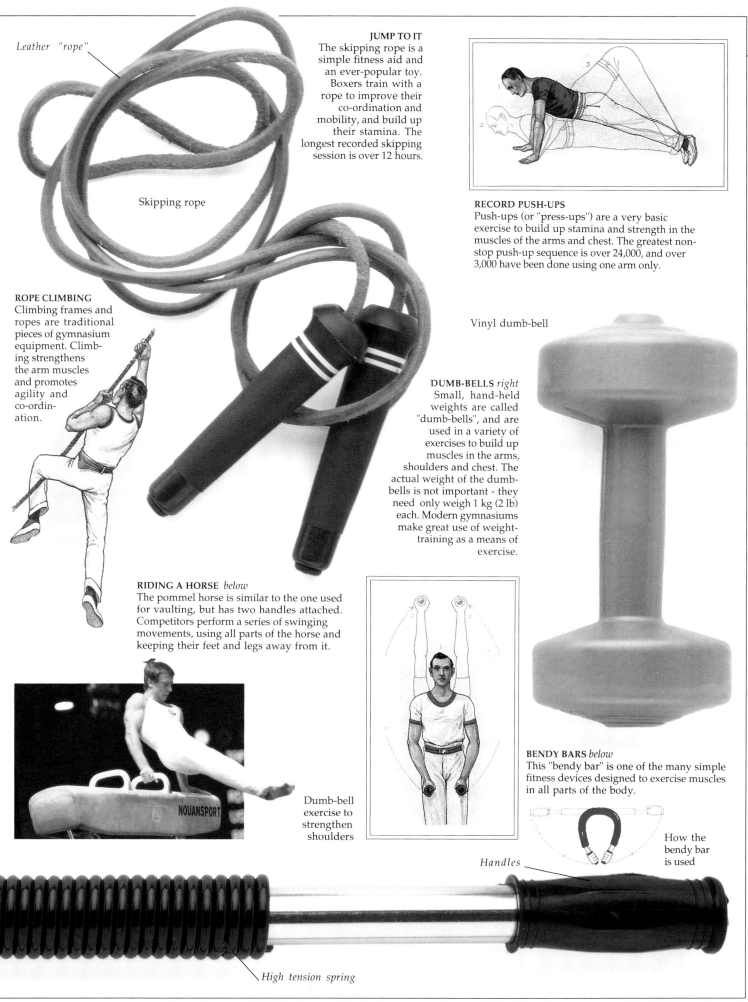

Leather "rope"

Skipping rope

JUMP TO IT
The skipping rope is a simple fitness aid and an ever-popular toy. Boxers train with a rope to improve their co-ordination and mobility, and build up their stamina. The longest recorded skipping session is over 12 hours.

RECORD PUSH-UPS
Push-ups (or "press-ups") are a very basic exercise to build up stamina and strength in the muscles of the arms and chest. The greatest non-stop push-up sequence is over 24,000, and over 3,000 have been done using one arm only.

ROPE CLIMBING
Climbing frames and ropes are traditional pieces of gymnasium equipment. Climbing strengthens the arm muscles and promotes agility and co-ordination.

Vinyl dumb-bell

DUMB-BELLS *right*
Small, hand-held weights are called "dumb-bells", and are used in a variety of exercises to build up muscles in the arms, shoulders and chest. The actual weight of the dumb-bells is not important - they need only weigh 1 kg (2 lb) each. Modern gymnasiums make great use of weight-training as a means of exercise.

RIDING A HORSE *below*
The pommel horse is similar to the one used for vaulting, but has two handles attached. Competitors perform a series of swinging movements, using all parts of the horse and keeping their feet and legs away from it.

NOUANSPORT

Dumb-bell exercise to strengthen shoulders

BENDY BARS *below*
This "bendy bar" is one of the many simple fitness devices designed to exercise muscles in all parts of the body.

Handles

How the bendy bar is used

High tension spring

Weightlifting

THE LIFTING OF WEIGHTS is one of the oldest and most simple forms of testing strength. Modern weightlifters compete against each other according to their body weight, as heavier men can usually lift the larger weights. In recent years, a great many people have discovered how training with weights helps build up the strength and stamina needed in other sports. Others use weights to develop muscles "for their own sake" and compete in special body-building contests.

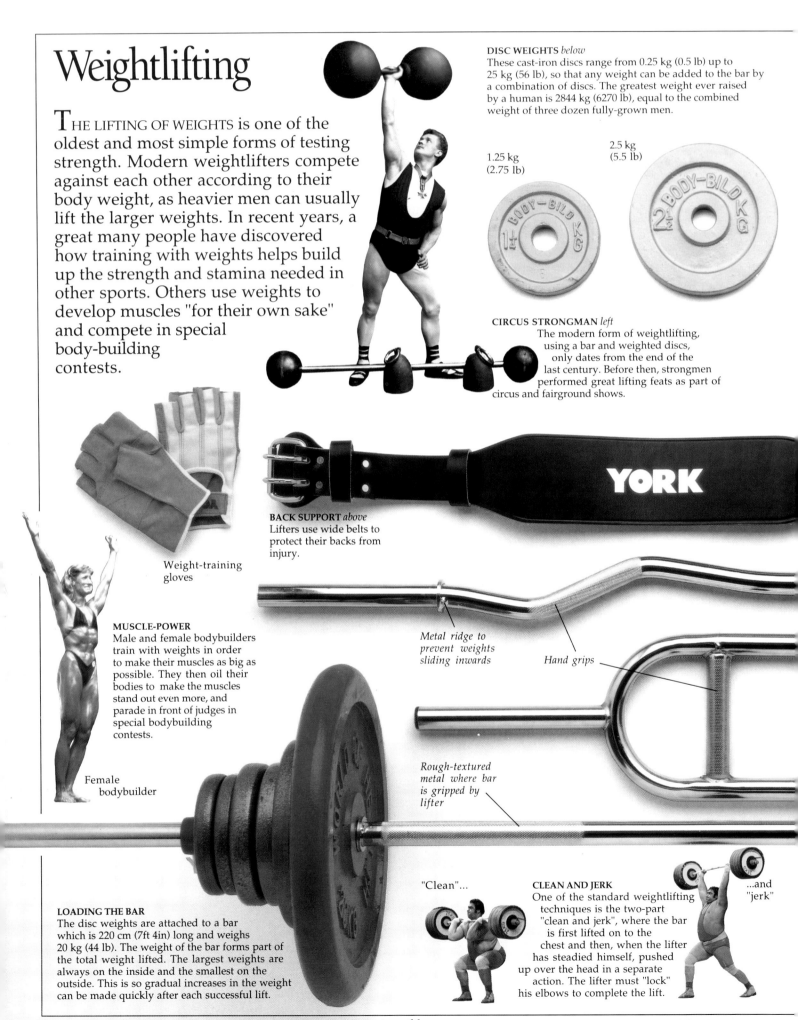

DISC WEIGHTS *below*
These cast-iron discs range from 0.25 kg (0.5 lb) up to 25 kg (56 lb), so that any weight can be added to the bar by a combination of discs. The greatest weight ever raised by a human is 2844 kg (6270 lb), equal to the combined weight of three dozen fully-grown men.

1.25 kg (2.75 lb)

2.5 kg (5.5 lb)

CIRCUS STRONGMAN *left*
The modern form of weightlifting, using a bar and weighted discs, only dates from the end of the last century. Before then, strongmen performed great lifting feats as part of circus and fairground shows.

BACK SUPPORT *above*
Lifters use wide belts to protect their backs from injury.

YORK

Weight-training gloves

MUSCLE-POWER
Male and female bodybuilders train with weights in order to make their muscles as big as possible. They then oil their bodies to make the muscles stand out even more, and parade in front of judges in special bodybuilding contests.

Female bodybuilder

Metal ridge to prevent weights sliding inwards

Hand grips

Rough-textured metal where bar is gripped by lifter

LOADING THE BAR
The disc weights are attached to a bar which is 220 cm (7ft 4in) long and weighs 20 kg (44 lb). The weight of the bar forms part of the total weight lifted. The largest weights are always on the inside and the smallest on the outside. This is so gradual increases in the weight can be made quickly after each successful lift.

"Clean"...

CLEAN AND JERK
One of the standard weightlifting techniques is the two-part "clean and jerk", where the bar is first lifted on to the chest and then, when the lifter has steadied himself, pushed up over the head in a separate action. The lifter must "lock" his elbows to complete the lift.

...and "jerk"

5 kg
(11 lb)

7.5 kg
(16.5 lb)

10 kg
(22 lb)

COLLARS
There are various
types of collar
that are used
to hold the
weights securely
on the bar.

Spring collar

Quick-release
collar

Screw-on
collar

PLASTIC WEIGHTS *right*
Rubber or plastic-covered weights
are normally used in top-class
competitions. These are usually
colour-coded, according to weight.
The 50 kg (110 lb) weights, which
are green, are only used if
there is no other way of
loading all the weight on
to the bar.

These plastic-covered dumb-bell weights are filled with sand

Bar for exercising
biceps (front upper
arms)

TYPES OF BARS *below*
Apart from the standard straight
bar, different-shaped bars are used for various
weight-training exercises. In these cases, the object
is not to lift the weights above the head, but to use
them to strengthen specific groups of muscles.

Bar for exercising
triceps (rear
upper arms)

Bar

Collar

*Small weights
on outside*

*Large weights
on inside*

SNATCH *right*
The other type of lift is
called the "snatch", in
which the bar is hoisted above
the head in one movement. It is
much harder to lift heavy
weights in this way. Contests
are decided by adding up the
weights lifted in the snatch
and clean-and-jerk.

POWERLIFTING
Powerlifters can
lift much
heavier
weights
than other
weightlifters,
but they do not have
to raise the bar
above their heads.

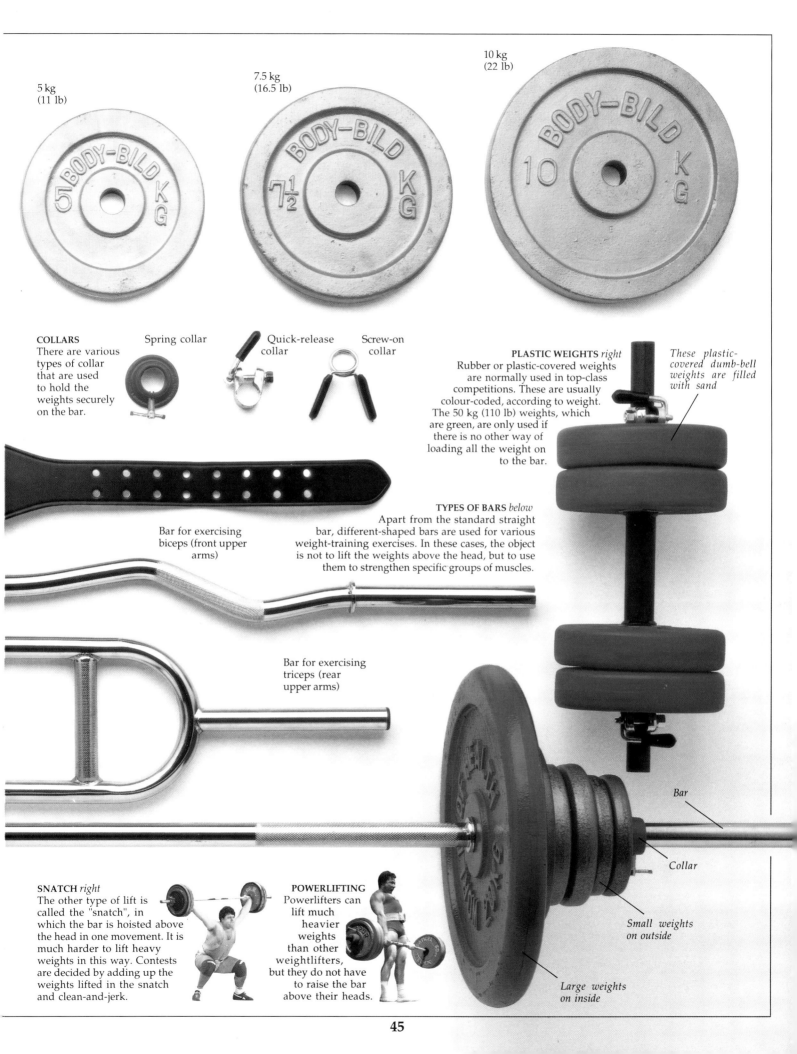

Boxing

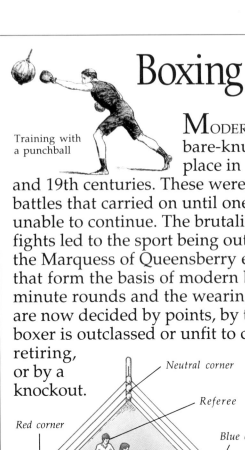

Training with a punchball

MODERN BOXING developed from the bare-knuckle prize-fights that took place in Britain during the 18th and 19th centuries. These were usually long, hard battles that carried on until one or both men were unable to continue. The brutality of these early fights led to the sport being outlawed but, in 1865, the Marquess of Queensberry established the rules that form the basis of modern boxing, with three-minute rounds and the wearing of gloves. Contests are now decided by points, by the referee deciding that a boxer is outclassed or unfit to continue the contest, by a boxer retiring, or by a knockout.

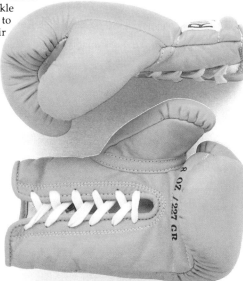

Dense foam rubber

Soft foam "sponge"

Cross-section of sparring glove

Wrist padding

BOXING GLOVES

Padded, lace-up gloves made of leather are worn on the bandaged hands. These normally weigh 227 g (8 oz) or 284 g (10 oz) depending on the boxer's weight. Bag gloves are worn when training with a punchbag or punchball.

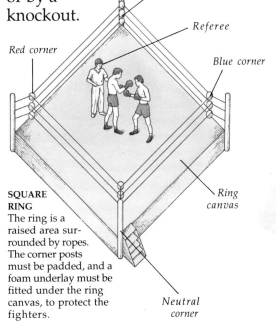

Neutral corner

Referee

Red corner

Blue corner

SQUARE RING
The ring is a raised area surrounded by ropes. The corner posts must be padded, and a foam underlay must be fitted under the ring canvas, to protect the fighters.

Ring canvas

Neutral corner

Bandaging the hands

HAND STRAPPING
Bare knuckle fighters used to "pickle" their hands in soda to make them hard. Nowadays, boxers use bandages on their hands for protection. Up to 5.6 m (18 ft) of soft bandage may be used by professional fighters.

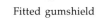

Adhesive tape

Fitted gumshield

Soft bandage

Competition gloves

Bag mitts

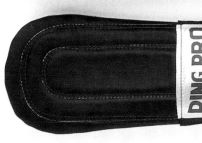

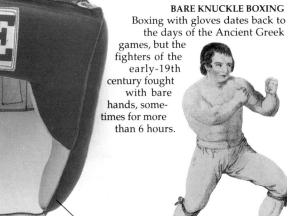

BARE KNUCKLE BOXING
Boxing with gloves dates back to the days of the Ancient Greek games, but the fighters of the early-19th century fought with bare hands, sometimes for more than 6 hours.

Bare knuckle fighter

Headguard

Chinstrap

Padded ear guards

**AMATEUR OR
PROFESSIONAL?** *above*
Amateur fights are fought
over three rounds of three
minutes each, compared to
up to 15 rounds for
professional championship
bouts. Amateurs always
wear vests, and may wear
the protective headguard
that professionals only use
when sparring (practising).
Every boxer wears a
gumshield, moulded to the
shape of his mouth, to
protect his teeth. A lace-up
protector is worn under the
shorts to guard against any
stray punches.

Elasticated belt

Boxing club
emblem embroidered
on to shorts

BOXING SHORTS
Boxers wear loose-fitting
shorts. Those used for
professional fights are
traditionally made from
satin, and often have the
name of the fighter or his
initials embroidered on
them. The "belt" is the line
between the top of the
boxer's hips and his
navel, and this must be
shown by a clear
contrast in colour.
Deliberately hitt-
ing "below the
belt" is
against the
rules.

Boxer's initials

The points system

The referee or judges award points to each boxer at the end
of every round. The maximum number of points
(normally 20) is given to the boxer who has
been most skilful in landing his punches
during that round; proportionately fewer
points are awarded to the other man. To
score points, a punch must be made with
the knuckle-part of the glove on the
front or sides of the opponent's head
or upper body. At the end of the
last round, the man with the
highest total of points is declared
the winner.

Direct left-hand blow to the body

FANCY FOOTWORK
The ability to move
quickly and smoothly
around the ring is an
important aspect of
boxing. Fighters prac-
tice their "dancing" with
a skipping rope, as part
of their training. The tall
boxing boots are light-
weight and have a thin
sole with no heel.

High sides provide
support for
boxer's ankles

Ducking to avoid left-hand punch and
countering with right-hand blow to jaw

Ducking to the right avoids left-hand
blow to the head

Thin flat sole

Lightweight
leather uppers

Martial arts

MARTIAL ARTS are those skills that are used in battle and, as such, could be applied to fencing, shooting and archery as well as to the sports described here. However, the term is usually used to describe the various combat sports that come from the Far East, of which judo and karate are the most widely practised. *Judo* means "the soft way", and involves throwing and holding movements. *Karate*, on the other hand, means "open hand", and is a mixture of punching and kicking techniques. The martial arts were first practised by the ancient Japanese *samurai* warriors, who were armed with bows and swords. The unarmed combat techniques, from which modern judo and karate evolved, enabled the warriors to continue fighting if they were suddenly disarmed by their opponent.

Film fighter Bruce Lee helped make the martial arts popular in the 1970s

KUNG FU WEAPONS
As well as the various forms of unarmed combat, martial artists learn to master weapons, such as the *nunchaku*, two wooden handles joined by a metal chain. This weapon developed from the rice flails used in the Chinese paddy fields. Sporting competitions use nunchaku with safe rubber handles.

Nunchaku

KENDO *below*
The traditional Japanese art of *kendo* is a form of fencing with wooden swords. The competitors, or *kendoka,* wear elaborate armour, and each bout lasts for just 3-5 minutes.

Leather hilt

Round "tsuba", or shield, is made of leather

Shinai

SUMO WRESTLING
The origins of Japanese *sumo* wrestling, in which contestants try to push each other out of the ring, date back to the 1st century B.C. The wrestlers put on weight by eating a high-protein stew - the heaviest ever wrestler weighed 225 kg (496 lb). Ritual is an important part of the sport.

Strong metal springs

Fingers hook over metal rings

Grip strengthener

Steel frame

GRIPPING STUFF
Martial arts fighters are supremely fit. Various devices, such as this grip strengthener, are used to build up strength and endurance. Agility and suppleness are also important - fighters train with special leg-stretchers which help them achieve high kicks.

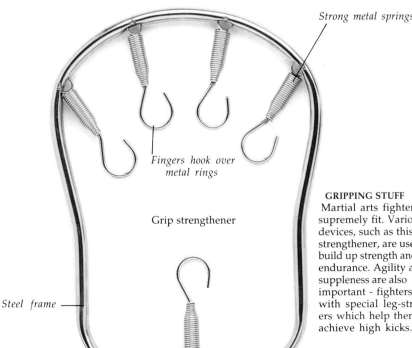

48

KENDO EQUIPMENT

The *kendoki* wear protective masks, gloves, breastplates and aprons. The kendo sword is called a *shinai* and is made from four strips of bamboo, lashed together with string and leather. It must be less than 118 cm (47 in) long.

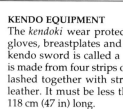

Leather tip

Bamboo strips

SELF-DEFENCE
Judo, karate and the other martial arts are practical forms of self-defence, as well as competitive sports.

Judo

Judo students are trained to make use of an opponent's strength to overcome him, while conserving their own energy. Sporting bouts are strictly controlled and the object is to display superior technique rather than to injure the opponent. Different levels of points are awarded according to the standard of throwing and holding movements.

SMASHING TECHNIQUE
The special physical and mental training of karate fighters enables them to break slabs of concrete and blocks of wood with their hands, feet or heads.

Karate

Karate contests normally last for two minutes, and are controlled by a referee and four judges. Actual physical contact is not required to score points - as with judo, it is superior technique that counts.

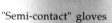
"Semi-contact" gloves

KARATE GLOVES
The many different forms of karate have different rules about protective clothing worn by the contestants, and the degree of physical contact allowed. Gloves of various kinds are sometimes used for sparring and in some competitions.

Foot protectors

FOOT PROTECTORS
These padded shoes slip over the bare feet of the fighter to protect his feet when delivering kicks to an opponent.

Red belt
9th-11th *dan*

Black belt
1st-5th *dan*

Brown belt
1st *kyu*

Blue belt
2nd *kyu*

Green belt
3rd *kyu*

Orange belt
4th *kyu*

Yellow belt
5th *kyu*

JUDO BELTS *right*
Fighters are awarded coloured belts to show the grade they have reached. The highest level reached by most people is the black belt, but there are three levels above this - red-and-white striped, red, and white belts.

Fencing

FENCING IS A COMBAT SPORT using swords, which takes place on a narrow "piste" 14 m (47 ft) long. The winner of a bout is the fencer who scores the greater number of "hits" on his opponent. The three types of modern sword - the *foil*, *épée* and *sabre* - are descendants of the *rapier*, which became the popular court weapon in the 16th century. The rapier and dagger replaced the heavier sword and "buckler" (shield) that had been carried before. Fencing swords do not have cutting blades and the tip is formed into a blunt button to prevent injuries.

16th-century duellist

METAL JACKET
In some contests, electronic equipment is used to show when a hit has been scored. Fencers have to wear special jackets covering the target area; these are made from woven metal threads, which conduct the electricity, so the scoreboard lights up when they are touched by the tip of the sword.

MESH MASK
The traditional mask protects the face and head, and a padded bib protects the throat. The fine mesh is made from stainless steel or moulded plastic. It allows the fencer to see out but prevents any accidental injuries to the eyes.

CLOTHING
The fencer's clothes must allow him freedom of movement and give maximum protection. They must be white, and made from stong material, and there must be no fastenings in which a sword may become caught.

GAUNTLET
A long white glove, or gauntlet, is worn only on the sword hand. It is slightly padded and extends halfway up the fencer's forearm.

Guard

Leather pad

"Tang"

Blade

Insert brass screw

Steel foil pommel

Alternative "pistol-grip" handle

THE SWORD
Swords are subject to strict rules governing their design and safety. The total length of any type of sword must not be more than 110 cm (44 in) - 105 cm (42 in) for the sabre.

Gripping the handle

THE BLADE
The blade is square in cross-section and has a groove running along its whole length. In electric-sword contests, the wire runs down this groove and is taped into place.

THE SABRE

The sabre may have a straight or curved blade but any curve must be continuous and less than 4 cm (1.5 in). The sword must weigh less than 500 g (1 lb) and the guard must measure no more than 15 cm x 14 cm (6 in x 5.5 in). Unlike the other swords, the edges of the sabre - as well as its tip - can be used to register hits.

THE FOIL

This light sword was developed especially for fencing practice in the 18th century. It weighs the same as the sabre, but its guard must have a diameter of no more than 12 cm (4.5 in). In electric foil contests, a hit registers only when pressure on the point is at least 500 g (1 lb).

THE EPEE

This is the traditional duelling sword, heavier than the foil and sabre, with a maximum weight of 750 g (1.5 lb) and a guard no larger than 13.5 cm (5.5 in) in diameter. A pressure of 750 g (1.5 lb) is needed to score a hit in electric épée bouts. Foils and épées usually have a strap, called a "martingale", attaching the sword to the fencer's hand.

DUELLISTS
The sport of fencing developed directly from the use of the sword in warfare and duelling. Gentlemen used to fight duels regularly as a way of settling "matters of honour", but these resulted in so many deaths that they were banned in many countries. Duellists often carried a sword in one hand and a dagger in the other.

The target area in sabre competitions is the trunk and arms

The target area for foil is the trunk, not including the arms

The target area for épée is the whole of the opponent's body

SWORD HILTS

The hilt of the modern sporting sabre most closely resembles those of duelling swords, which were designed to protect the sword hand.

Modern sabre hilt

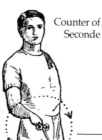

Cavalry dragoon c. 1840

Martingale

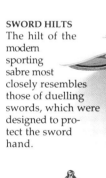

16th century rapier hilt

CAVALRY CHARGE
The sabre used in modern fencing competition is a light version of the sword used by cavalry troops in the 18th and 19th centuries. The weapon was especially designed for use by troops on horseback and had a flat, curved blade.

USING ELECTRICITY
Official foil and épée competitions always use an electric scoring system in which the sword tips are connected to lights, by a long wire which passes underneath each fencer's jacket.

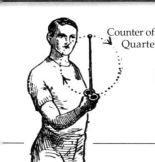 Counter of Quarte
 Counter of Sixte
 Counter of Septime
 Counter of Seconde

FENCING TECHNIQUE
These circular movements - which are made by moving the fingers and wrist only - are used to deflect the opponent's blade. Many of the fencing terms date from the 16th or 17th century, when the light court sword was introduced in France.

 Button

Archery

VARIOUS FORMS of bow and arrow have been used to fight battles and as hunting tools for thousands of years. Modern sporting bows are designed and made according to the same principles, although the sights, stabilizers and other attachments make them look very different. Competitors in target archery shoot a certain number of arrows at targets fixed at different distances - 30 m, 50 m, 70 m and 90 m for men, and 30 m, 50 m, 60 m and 70 m for women. The points scored are added up to give a total, and the archer with the highest total is the winner. Crossbows are sometimes used in separate competitions.

Cupid's arrows cause people to fall in love

THE BAYEAUX TAPESTRY
Archers and slingers used to be less effective in battle than an army's main forces of cavalry and foot soldiers (infantry), until the introduction of the longbow in the Middle Ages.

The dacron string is taken off the bow after each shooting session

Hardwood laminate limbs

"Riser"

VICTORIAN ARCHERS
The bows used by 19th-century archers were usually made from two pieces of wood, joined (spliced) together in the centre. Those made from a single piece are called "self bows".

PROTECTION
A "bracer" is worn on the arm that holds the bow, to protect it against the bowstring. A glove or finger tab is worn on the drawing hand.

THE MODERN BOW
Until recently, bows were always made from wood, the best being yew. Modern bows are usually made from laminates and other materials, such as fibreglass and carbon. These are much stronger and therefore more reliable.

Finger tab

Sight ring attachment

BOWSIGHT *left*
A sight can be fixed to the side of the bow, to help the archer concentrate his aim.

Magnesium handle

Archer's glove

Bracer

STABILIZERS *below*
These are screwed into the "risers" to make the bow more stable while shooting, so each shot is consistent.

The "nock" rests on the string

There are three feather "fletches" on each arrow

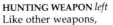

"V-bar" stabilizers

HUNTING WEAPON *left*
Like other weapons, the bow and arrow was first used to help man catch his food. In the case of the Red Indians, it was used to kill buffalo which also provided hides to make clothing and shelter.

MINI ARROWS
Crossbows fire "bolts", which are much shorter than arrows but must be at least 30 cm (12 in) long.

Laminated fibreglass bow

ARCHERY TARGET *right*
Paper target faces are pinned to straw "butts". Each of the five coloured rings has an inner and an outer part, making ten areas in all. Points from 1 to 10 are scored depending on how close the arrows are to the centre of the target - the "bull's eye".

Straw butt

White (inner) 2 points

Blue (outer) 5 points

Bolt rests in groove

String held back in loosing position here

Aiming sight

Stirrup held between feet when drawing bow

THE CROSSBOW
Like a cross between a bow and a gun, the crossbow is held like a rifle and the string released by a trigger. The "stock" of the weapon is usually made of hardwood, such as walnut, and the actual bow of fibreglass or some similar material.

WILLIAM TELL
The legendary Swiss hero William Tell was ordered to shoot an apple off his young son's head as a punishment. The legend usually says that he used a crossbow, but this picture shows him with a longbow.

Metal tip

THE PARTS OF AN ARROW *above*
The craft of making arrows is known as "fletching". Cedar and red deal are the woods traditionally used to make the best arrows.

Wooden shaft

THE QUIVER *right*
This is the "holster" which holds the arrows, and is usually worn on a belt around the archer's waist. The arrows in this quiver have aluminium shafts and plastic fletches.

LONGSHOT *left*
Modern bows are very powerful. A "footbow", in which the arrow is drawn back with both hands, can shoot an arrow over 1800 m (well over a mile). The record for a handbow is over 1100 m (3600 ft).

Aluminium longrod stabilizer

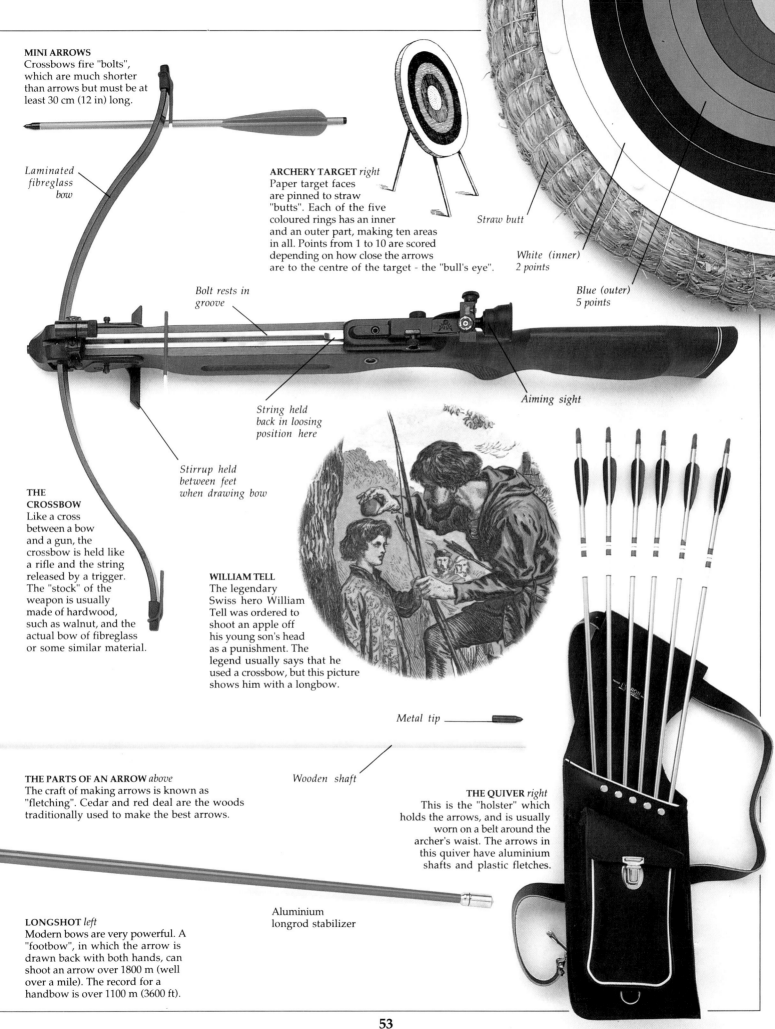

Shooting

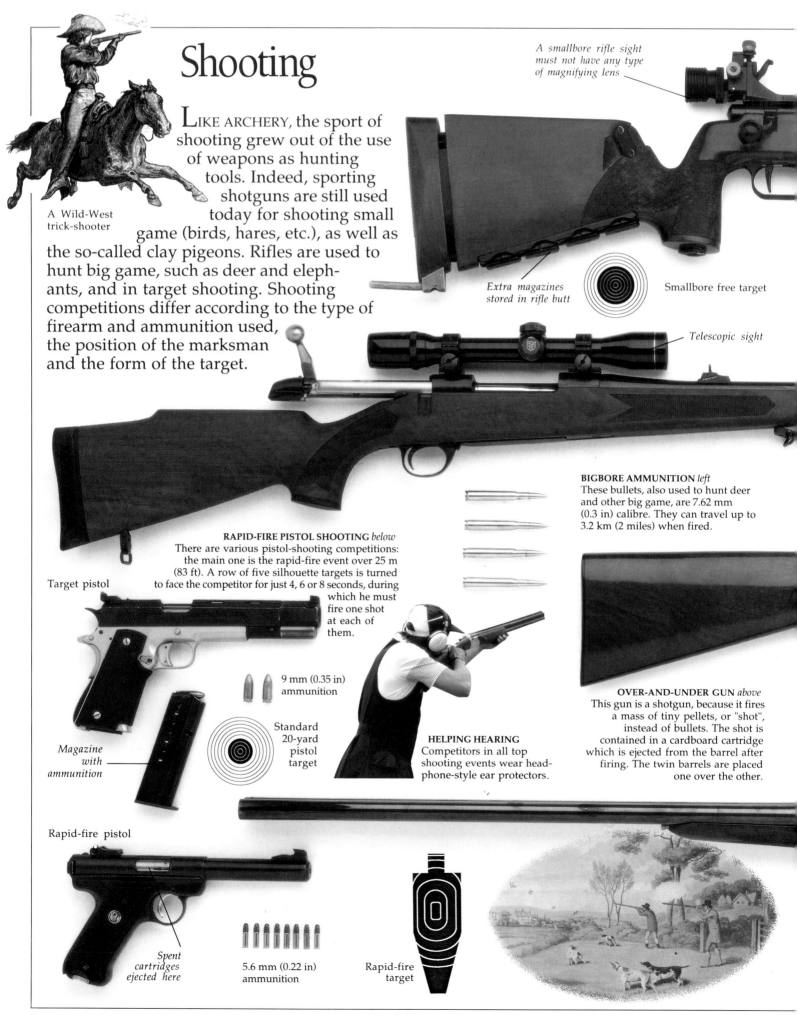

LIKE ARCHERY, the sport of shooting grew out of the use of weapons as hunting tools. Indeed, sporting shotguns are still used today for shooting small game (birds, hares, etc.), as well as the so-called clay pigeons. Rifles are used to hunt big game, such as deer and elephants, and in target shooting. Shooting competitions differ according to the type of firearm and ammunition used, the position of the marksman and the form of the target.

A Wild-West trick-shooter

A smallbore rifle sight must not have any type of magnifying lens

Extra magazines stored in rifle butt

Smallbore free target

Telescopic sight

BIGBORE AMMUNITION *left*
These bullets, also used to hunt deer and other big game, are 7.62 mm (0.3 in) calibre. They can travel up to 3.2 km (2 miles) when fired.

RAPID-FIRE PISTOL SHOOTING *below*
There are various pistol-shooting competitions: the main one is the rapid-fire event over 25 m (83 ft). A row of five silhouette targets is turned to face the competitor for just 4, 6 or 8 seconds, during which he must fire one shot at each of them.

Target pistol

9 mm (0.35 in) ammunition

Standard 20-yard pistol target

Magazine with ammunition

HELPING HEARING
Competitors in all top shooting events wear head-phone-style ear protectors.

OVER-AND-UNDER GUN *above*
This gun is a shotgun, because it fires a mass of tiny pellets, or "shot", instead of bullets. The shot is contained in a cardboard cartridge which is ejected from the barrel after firing. The twin barrels are placed one over the other.

Rapid-fire pistol

Spent cartridges ejected here

5.6 mm (0.22 in) ammunition

Rapid-fire target

SMALLBORE FREE RIFLE *below*
This weapon is fired from a distance of 50 m (165 ft) at a round target 16.24 cm (6.5 in) across. The diameter, or "calibre", of the bullets used is 5.6 mm (0.22 in).

Barrel sight

Ammunition for smallbore free rifle

THE BIATHLON
This is a modern sport combining cross-country skiing and rifle shooting. Competitors ski a course of up to 20 km (12.5 miles) and stop for three or four sessions of shooting at targets from a range of 150 m (495 ft).

ANNIE GET YOUR GUN
The remarkable Annie Oakley was a famous trick-shooter: as part of her act, she would shoot a cigarette from between the lips of her husband, and split a playing card from a distance of 30 paces.

BIGBORE RIFLE *above*
This hunting rifle is fired over a distance of 300 m (1000 ft) at a target 1 m (39 in) across. The term "rifle" refers to the spiral-shaped groove inside the barrel of the guns that causes the bullets to spin through the air as they are fired.

Air-pistol pellets

Over-and-under barrels

AIR WEAPONS
Air pistols and rifles use compressed air or carbon dioxide to fire tiny pellets from a range of 10 m (33 ft) at targets just 4.6 cm (1.8 in) across. These pellets have to be loaded one at a time.

The wooden grip is specially shaped to fit the hand exactly

Cartridge

Pellets

"BB" 4.3 mm (0.172 in) shot

"No.9" 2.0 mm (0.08 in) shot

TYPES OF SHOT
Different sizes of shot are used for different purposes. Large pellets travel further and are used to shoot birds, but smaller pellets scatter over a wide area more quickly and are used in clay-pigeon shooting.

CLAY PIGEONS
These small, saucer-shaped clay discs are launched two at a time from special traps on the ground, so their flight resembles that of game birds.

A traditional hunting scene left

SIDE-BY-SIDE GUN *above*
This traditional sporting gun is used to shoot small game birds. Its barrels are alongside each other rather than "over-and-under". Special "gun dogs" are trained to retrieve birds which have been shot by their masters.

Bowling sports

THERE ARE TWO main kinds of bowling sports: those in which the object is to knock down pins or skittles, and those in which the players try to get their bowls nearer to the target ball, or jack, than their opponent. The modern form of tenpin bowling was "invented" when the game of skittles - which had nine pins arranged in a "diamond" formation - was banned in the United States in 1845; the players merely added another pin and rearranged them into a triangle.

Crown-green bowls jack

Boule

BOULES *above*
The sport of boules, or petanque, is played mainly by the French. The heavy metal spheres are rolled or thrown at a small wooden jack. The pitch usually has a sandy surface.

Crown-green bowls foot mat ("footer")

Crown-green bowl, or "wood"

Boules technique

Bowls technique

CROWN-GREEN BOWLS *above*
This game is played on a square grass lawn that is raised slightly to form a "crown" in the centre. The jack is larger than the one used in the more popular flat-green version.

BOWLING TECHNIQUES *above*
The object of bowls and boules is the same, but boules can be thrown while bowls must always be rolled along the ground. Each bowl is weighted or "biased" on one side so that it curves gently when it is rolled.

Flat-green wood

BOWLING SHOES
These have flat soles to avoid damaging the green.

Flat-green jack

FLAT-GREEN BOWLS
Traditionally, each set of four bowls, or "woods", was made from a single log of the heavy wood *lignum vitae*. The black or brown bowls are now often made from rubber or composition materials instead.

SIR FRANCIS DRAKE
The English admiral Sir Francis Drake is believed to have been playing a form of bowls at Plymouth when the Spanish invasion fleet, or "Armada", was sighted in 1588.

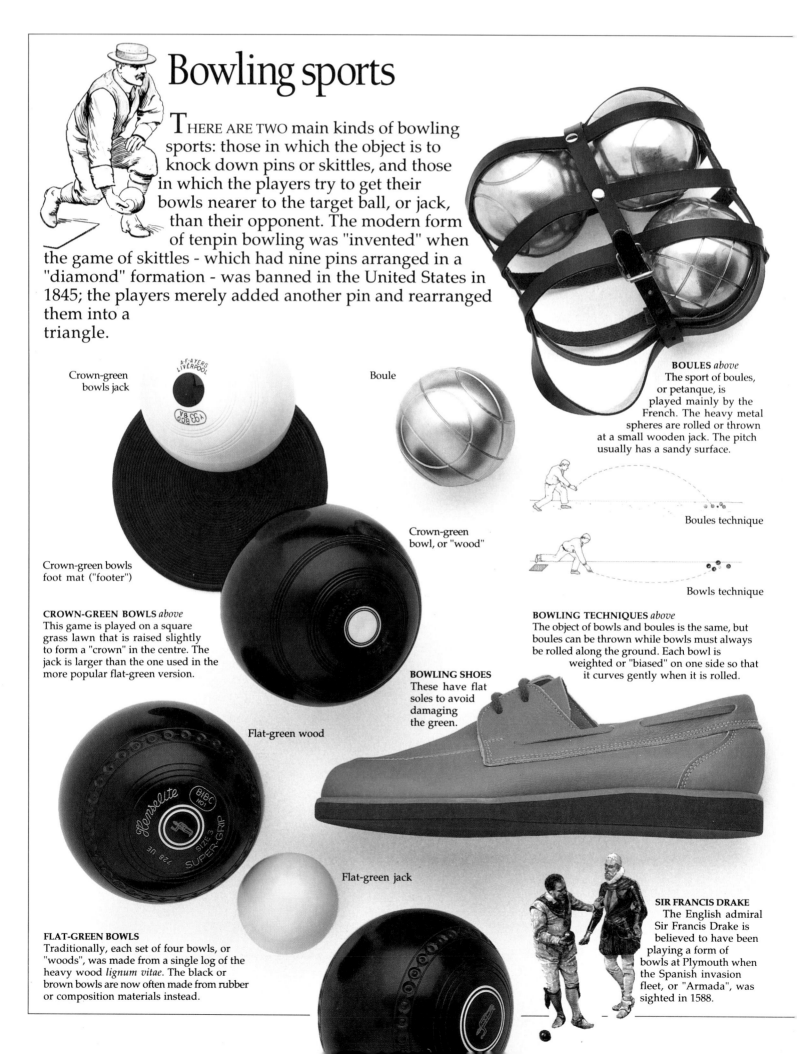

A MEDIEVAL BOWLING GAME
Games in which balls are thrown or rolled along the ground towards a target are among the oldest and most popular of all, dating back to the days of the ancient Egyptians.

MARBLES *below*
Roman children used to play a game like marbles, flicking nuts into an area marked on the floor. There are many different forms of the sport, using balls made from glass or baked clay.

Marbles

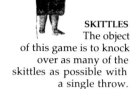

SKITTLES
The object of this game is to knock over as many of the skittles as possible with a single throw.

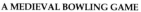

Most bowlers use a three-finger grip

Brunswick
GRM2688
Black Beauty

Bowling ball

THE LANE
The pins are set out in a triangular pattern at the far end of the lane, which may be made from plastic or thin strips of pine or maple wood.

TENPIN BOWLING
Bowlers roll the heavy ball down a narrow lane, and try to knock down the pins at the other end. Points are scored for each pin knocked down. The ball is made from hard rubber composition or plastic, and may weigh up to 7.26 kg (16 lb). Finger holes are drilled into the ball to make gripping easier.

Pins

CURLING *above*
This is a bowling sport on ice; players slide round "stones" towards a target area called a "house". Brushes are used to sweep away frost and moisture from in front of the running stone. This helps to keep it straight and makes it go further.

Curling stone

THE PINS
The ten pins are made from maple wood, and covered in plastic to protect them against the impact of the ball. Each pin stands on a numbered spot within the formation.

Golf

THE ORIGINS OF GOLF are not clear, but it almost certainly belongs to the same family of sports as bowling and croquet. The modern form of the game was first played in Scotland some 400 years ago. Golfers hit a small ball with clubs from a starting point ("tee") into a hole located some distance away. Modern golf courses have eighteen holes, and the object is to hit the ball into each hole, and so complete the round, using as few strokes as possible.

GOLF CLUBS
A player may use no more than 14 different clubs in any round of golf. Most players use three or four wooden clubs ("woods"), nine or ten metal clubs ("irons") and a "putter". The ball must only be hit with the head of the club.

WOODS
These clubs have large heads made from wood, or sometimes plastic or metal, and have longer shafts than other clubs. They are capable of hitting the ball a long way, and are used for the first tee-shot - the "drive" - and for other long shots. The most commonly-used woods are numbered 1 to 5. A number 1 wood, known as the "driver", is the largest.

Number 1 wood

Number 3 wood

Number 5 wood

CLUB HEADS
Wooden clubs are made from persimmon or laminates of other woods. Face inserts and metal sole-plates help prevent the club being damaged.

THE SWING *left*
The ball is placed on a small wooden or plastic tee, which raises it off the ground. The golfer takes a great swing at the ball, following through with his club. Hitting the ball straight into the hole from the tee is a "hole in one".

Practice ball

Golf ball

Tee

GOLF BALLS
These are covered in over 400 "dimples", which help the ball fly long and straight when hit. Players use lightweight "airballs" to practise their technique.

A TYPICAL HOLE *below*
The length of a hole may be between 100-600 m (300-2000 ft). This length determines its "par" - the number of strokes normally needed to get the ball into the hole. If a player completes a hole in a shot less than par, he scores a "birdie", two shots less scores an "eagle", and three shots less an "albatross". The length and features of each course vary a great deal.

The "tee" is a smooth level area from which the first shot is taken

Club head —

METAL WOODS
Some woods are not wooden at all, but made from metal or plastic.

Shaft

HEADCOVERS
Special sleeves protect the heads of clubs from the weather when they are not being used.

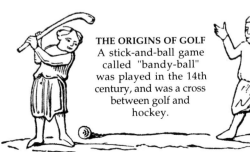

THE ORIGINS OF GOLF
A stick-and-ball game called "bandy-ball" was played in the 14th century, and was a cross between golf and hockey.

IRONS

The heads of the metal clubs are narrower than the woods; they are made from chromium-plated steel, and used for shorter shots. The irons are numbered 1 to 10. The head of each is angled differently for different kinds of shot - a number 1 iron hits the ball further and lower than a number 2, and so on.

Number 2 iron (18 degree angle)

Number 3 iron (21 degree angle)

Number 4 iron (24 degree angle)

Number 5 iron (27 degree angle)

Number 6 iron (31 degree angle)

Number 7 iron (35 degree angle)

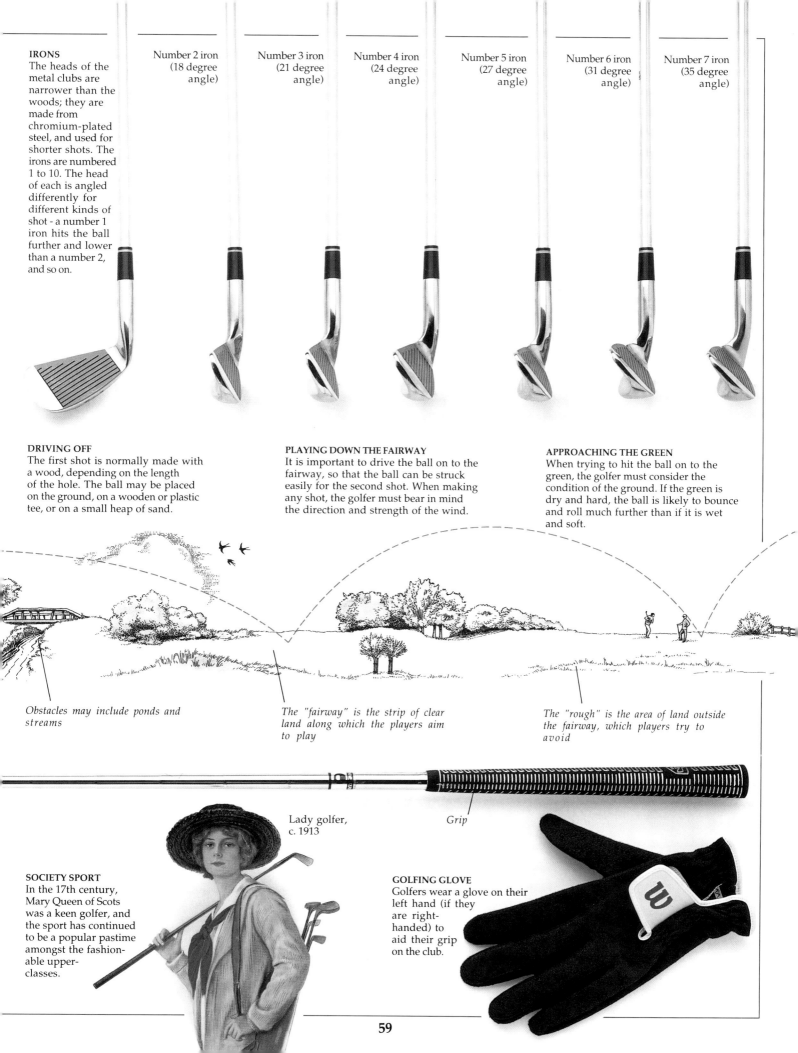

DRIVING OFF
The first shot is normally made with a wood, depending on the length of the hole. The ball may be placed on the ground, on a wooden or plastic tee, or on a small heap of sand.

PLAYING DOWN THE FAIRWAY
It is important to drive the ball on to the fairway, so that the ball can be struck easily for the second shot. When making any shot, the golfer must bear in mind the direction and strength of the wind.

APPROACHING THE GREEN
When trying to hit the ball on to the green, the golfer must consider the condition of the ground. If the green is dry and hard, the ball is likely to bounce and roll much further than if it is wet and soft.

Obstacles may include ponds and streams

The "fairway" is the strip of clear land along which the players aim to play

The "rough" is the area of land outside the fairway, which players try to avoid

Lady golfer, c. 1913

Grip

SOCIETY SPORT
In the 17th century, Mary Queen of Scots was a keen golfer, and the sport has continued to be a popular pastime amongst the fashionable upper-classes.

GOLFING GLOVE
Golfers wear a glove on their left hand (if they are right-handed) to aid their grip on the club.

59

Pitching wedge, used to "chip" the ball on to the green (48 degree angle)

Sand wedge, used to get the ball out of a bunker (55 degree angle)

PUTTERS
Putters are light clubs, usually made of metal, which are used only on the putting green. They have flat faces but come in many different designs to suit each player's taste.

Standard centre-shaft putter

Large-head putter with angled neck

Small-head centre-shaft putter

GETTING OUT OF TROUBLE
If the ball is accidentally hit into a bunker, it can be very difficult to get out. A sand wedge may be used to "lift" the ball on to the green.

PUTTING
Once the ball is on the green, a putter is used to hit it along the ground and into the hole.

THE PUTTING TECHNIQUE
The ball must be struck with the head of the club - not pushed or "scraped" along the ground. The golfer must take into account the direction of any slope when making his stroke.

Sand-pits, or "bunkers", are often placed close to the green

The "green" is the closely mown area of grass where the hole is located

The hole is marked with a flag, known as the "pin"

BALL MARKERS
On the green, players may pick up their ball and mark its position with a small disc while an opponent takes his putt.

GOLF SHOES
Golfers wear shoes with spiked soles to help them stand firm when they are swinging their clubs. The most expensive pair of shoes in the world are mink-lined golf shoes with gold trim and ruby-tipped spikes.

THE CADDIE
The caddie is an assistant who carries the bag of clubs around the course. This is an 18th-century caddie.

60

Croquet

Croquet has much in common with lawn bowls (p. 56) but, like golf, the sport involves hitting a ball at a target with a club - or, in this case, a "mallet". A game consists of scoring points by hitting coloured balls through a series of arches, or "hoops", in a certain order. The secret of the sport is to keep the balls of your own side close together, and those of the opposing side as far apart as possible. The winner is the player or team who gets all their balls to the end of the course first.

PEGGING OUT
The balls must be hit through each of the six hoops twice, and a point is scored for each hoop. At the end of the course, the player hits the ball against the wooden peg to score an extra point, making a total of 13 for each ball.

A BYGONE AGE
Croquet, like golf, was a fashionable social pastime during the Victorian era. The popularity of the sport declined as lawn tennis (p. 30) became "all the rage" in the late-19th century, but is now enjoying a revival.

The handle of the mallet is usually made of ash

THE TEN-HOOP GAME
Modern croquet matches use just six hoops, but the old-fashioned form of the game used ten. The broad, round-topped hoops used at that time were thought to be much too easy to get the ball through, so they were replaced with the modern narrower kind.

HOOPS
The iron hoops are just wide enough for the balls to pass through. They are painted white, and the crown of the last hoop, the "rover", is red.

THE BALLS
Each player or team plays with two of the four balls, which are traditionally made from boxwood or composite material.

MALLETS
Players must hit the ball, rather than push it, with the head of the mallet, which is about 80 cm (32 in) long from the tip of the handle to the base of the head.

THE CROQUET SHOT
If a player hits his ball into another ball, he is allowed to make a "croquet" shot. He places his ball against the other ball and hits it so that both balls are sent in different directions.

SINGLES AND DOUBLES
Two players may compete with two balls each, or four players can compete as two teams, with one ball per player. Each player must use the same coloured ball throughout the game. Blue and black always play against red and yellow.

The boxwood mallet head may be square or cylindrical

HOCKEY ON HORSEBACK
The sport of polo is like a cross between hockey (p. 16) and croquet, played by teams of four riders on horseback. Long-handled mallets made from sycamore or ash are used to hit a ball towards goals set 275 m (900 ft) apart.

Pool and snooker

THESE INDOOR SPORTS are played on a rectangular table that has "pockets" at the corners and in the middle of the longest sides. Players use long wooden cues to hit balls into the pockets and score points or, in the case of the "8-ball" version of pool, they try to "pot" their set of balls before their opponent pots his set. Both sports evolved from the game of billiards, which dates back to around the 15th century, when it was probably played outdoors on grass. King Louis XI of France is thought to have been the first to play the game indoors.

THE ROYAL MACE
Billiards was popular at the French court at Versailles. Players in Louis XIV's day had to hit the ball with a "mace" - a stick some 1 m (3 ft) long, flattened at one end into a spoon shape.

Over 56 km (35 miles) of woollen yarn are needed to cover a 4 m x 2 m (12 ft 6in x 6ft 7in) table

THE TABLE
The first tables were made from oak and marble, and the modern slate-bed tables were not introduced until the 1830s. The use of the rigid slate ensures that the playing surface is completely flat. The table is covered with a fine-quality woollen cloth.

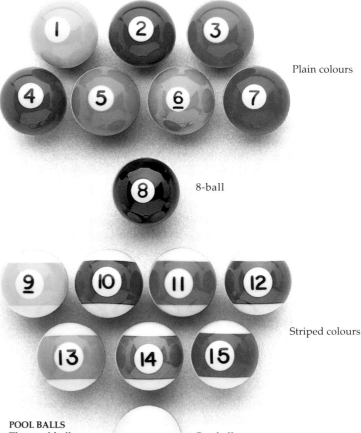

Plain colours

8-ball

Striped colours

Cue ball

Slate bed screwed to wooden underframe

POCKETS
Balls that fall into the holes are collected in string pockets.

POOL BALLS
The pool balls are divided into two groups - numbers 1-7 are solid colours, and numbers 9-15 are striped. In "8-ball" pool, each player must pocket all the balls in one of these groups and then pot the black 8-ball to win.

Two-piece cues have a screw attachment

Snooker

The game of snooker was invented by a British Army officer in India in 1875. The term "snooker" was a nickname for military cadets in England at the time. Players score points by potting the red balls, after which they may attempt a coloured ball, which is worth more points. Potted coloured balls are replaced on their spots until no reds are left. The players then try to pot the coloured balls in a certain order, finishing with the black ball.

Cue ball

Brown ball (4 points)

Green ball (3 points)

Yellow ball (2 points)

Blue ball (5 points)

Pink ball (6 points)

THE SNOOKER *left*
A player is "snookered" if the direct path to the object ball is blocked by another ball.

Object ball

Cue ball

Position of the balls at the start of play

Rubber "cushions" along each edge of the table

Cue ball struck from within this area at the start of each "frame"

The bridge

CUEING ACTION
The player makes his shot by leaning over the table and resting the cue on a "bridge" formed with the fingers of his front hand.

SNOOKER BALLS
There are fifteen red balls, six other colours and a white cue ball. At the start of each game, or frame, the coloured balls are placed on their spots and the red balls are arranged using a wooden triangle.

Red balls (1 point)

Triangle

Black ball (7 points)

BAGATELLE BOARD
Bagatelle is one of a number of games developed to be played on tables. In this version, played on a table 2-3 m (6-10 ft) long, balls are rolled into numbered holes; pins, arches and bells were added in some cases, making this the forerunner of the modern pinball machine.

TAKING A REST
The position of the cue ball may sometimes make it difficult or impossible for a player to form a normal bridge. In such cases, a rest may be used: there are various kinds for different situations.

Standard rest

Extended "spider" rest

"Spider" rest

THE CUE
Cues may be one-piece or two-piece, and are normally made from ash or Canadian maple wood and South American hardwoods, such as ebony. The domed tip is made from leather.

CHALK CUBE
Chalk is rubbed on to the cue tip to improve contact with the ball.

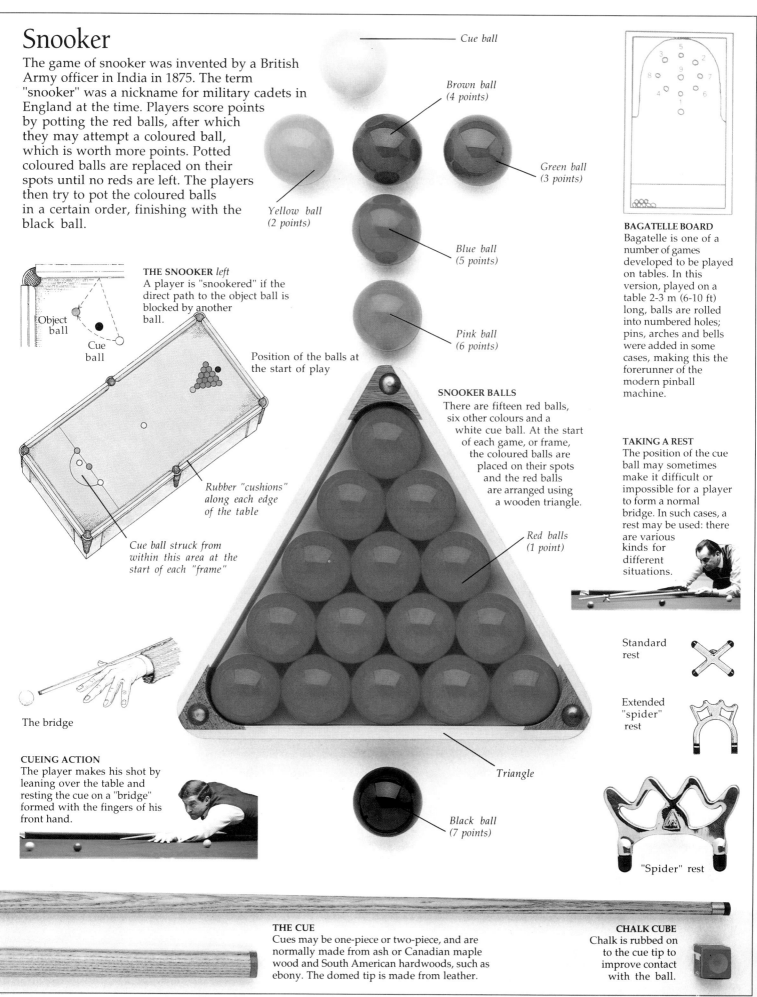

Index

Acknowledgments

Dorling Kindersley would like to thank:
Grandstand Sports and Leisure
Geron Way
Edgware Road
London NW2

A & D Billiards & Pool Services Ltd, Amateur Athletics Association, Amateur Boxing Association, Amateur Fencing Association, Badminton Association of England Ltd, Bapty and Co. Ltd, Billiards and Snooker Control Council, British Amateur Baseball and Softball Federation, British Amateur Weight Lifters' Association, British American Football Association, British Ice Hockey Federation, British Racketball Association, British Tenpin Bowling Association, Jonathan Buckley, Continental Sports Products Co., The Croquet Association, Dragon Martial Arts, English Basketball Association, English Bowling Association, English Table Tennis Association, The Football Association, The Football League Ltd, C.L. Gaul & Co. Ltd, James Gilbert Ltd, Grand National Archery Society, Grays of Cambridge (International) Ltd, Gridiron Sports, International Hockey Federation, Quicks the Archery Specialist, Leon Paul Equipment Co. Ltd, Charlie Magri Sports, Martial Arts Commission, Marylebone Cricket Club, Minerva Football Co. Ltd, Diana Morgan, Newitt & Co. Ltd, Professional Golfers Association, The Rugby Football Union, Len Smiths (School & Sports) Ltd, Squash Rackets Association, Wilson Sporting Goods Co. Ltd, Wimbledon Lawn Tennis Museum.

Ray Owen for artwork

Polyflex running-track materials (pp. 3 and 39) used by courtesy of Recreational Surfaces Ltd

Picture credits
t=top b=bottom m=middle l=left r=right

All-sport (UK): 6tr, bm; 7m; 9b; 10t, mr; 11tr; 13tm, ml; 14br; 16ml; 18tr; 19tm, br; 20tl, bl; 21bl; 23bm; 26mr; 27m; 35ml, bl, 36bl; 37ml; 38tl, bl; 39tl, m; 40tr, br; 47tl; 48bl, mr; 50bl; 52br; 55tl; 61b; 63mr, bl.
BBC Hulton Picture Library: 10br; 13br; 18tl; 22tr, bl; 25bl; 28ml; 38ml; 40bl; 44tm; 50tl; 51tr, m; 52bl; 53m; 54tl; 55tr; 57tl, tr; 62tr.
The British Library: 54br.
The British Museum: 49tm.
Colorsport/SIPA: 7tm, tr; 9m; 14tr; 15tl; 24bl; 27tl; 31tr, ml; 34m; 42tr, bl; 43bl; 44ml, bm, br; 45bl, bm; 49m; 54m; 58ml. The Mansell Collection: 34bm; 35br; 56br; 58br.
Mary Evans Picture Library: 8t; 14tl, ml; 15mr; 16tr; 17mr; 25tl, br; 26tl, m; 30br; 31tl; 32tl; 34tl; 37br; 39bl; 41ml, bm; 46bm; 52tl, tr, mr; 57bl; 59bl; 60bl; 61ml.

Cigarette card illustrations on pp. 42-3 reproduced courtesy of W.D & H.O. Wills

Illustrations by Will Giles: 10m, bl; 30ml; 35tl; 38mr; 40tr; 57m; 62bl; 63ml.

Illustrations by Sandra Pond: 6m; 13tr, m; 16mr; 19tl; 20mr; 21bl; 22bl; 24mr; 26tr; 39m; 40b; 46ml, m; 51m.

Illustration by Coral Mula: 58-60m.

Picture research by:
Joanne King

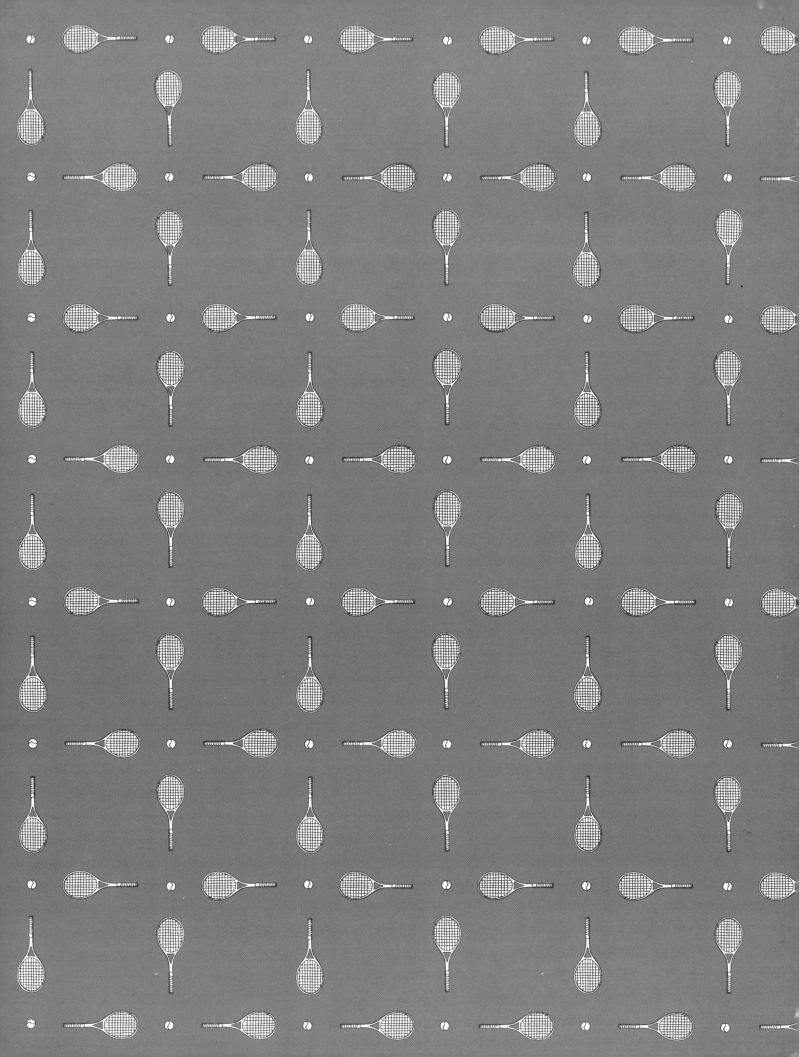